T0277562

# BLACK THEOLOGY AND BLACK FAITH

# BLACK THEOLOGY AND BLACK FAITH

Noel Leo Erskine

WILLIAM B. EERDMANS PUBLISHING COMPANY
GRAND RAPIDS, MICHIGAN

Wm. B. Eerdmans Publishing Co.
4035 Park East Court SE, Grand Rapids, Michigan 49546
www.eerdmans.com

Book design by Leah Luyk

Printed in the United States of America

29  28  27  26  25  24  23      1  2  3  4  5  6  7

ISBN 978-0-8028-7560-0

**Library of Congress Cataloging-in-Publication Data**

A catalog record for this book is available from the Library of Congress.

*For my students and colleagues at*
*Emory University*

# Contents

# Preface

This book contends that the Black religious experience emerged and unfolded in the Caribbean and South America and not in the United States of America. Of the eleven million Africans who survived the Middle Passage and were forced to work on plantations in the New World, only about 450,000 arrived in the United States. All the rest went to the Caribbean and South America. This explains the numerical advantage Black people in the Caribbean had over their counterparts in the United States. Because many Caribbean nations are made up of more than 90 percent Afro-Caribbean people, Black people there have the confidence to protest and the luxury of majority thinking. Because of this numerical advantage, Caribbean people were able to preserve their stories and traditions. The memory of Africa lingers and is manifest in culture, especially at points where faith and history meet.

Both the historical priority and the cultural and political majority of enslaved persons in the Caribbean allow the Caribbean experience to frame much of the discussion and the understanding of Black faith that emerges.

This book presses beyond the nation-state framework and raises intercultural and interregional questions with implications for gender, race, and class. This comparative analysis allows the rethinking of the language and grammar of how Black faith has been understood in the Americas and extends the notion of Black theology and Black faith beyond the United States of America. The forging of Black faith from sources African and European presses the meaning of Black theology and Black faith when people of African descent are culturally and politically in the majority. The converse is pertinent. What is the meaning of Black theology and Black faith when people of African descent are a cultural and political minority?

Chapter 1 highlights suffering and multiple forms of oppression as the soil in which Black faith comes to life. The work of Michelle Alexander in *The New Jim Crow* is of first importance, as she informs us that the current prison population in the United States far exceeds the number of Africans and people of African descent who were brought to American colonies as enslaved persons. Voices from Cuba, Martinique, Guadeloupe, and Jamaica join in conversation concerning the scope and shape of Black faith in these regions. Contributions of Malcolm X, Bob Marley, and Marcus Garvey are highlighted.

In the context of New World slavery, Black people were sinned against. The sin of slavery was the rupture of ancestors from self, family, land, religion, and way of life. In chapter 2 much attention is given to the meaning of sin and its gesture toward life and reconciliation. The framing of the exposition of sin and reconciliation is advanced by Dorothee Sölle, Bob Marley, and J. Deotis Roberts. Both Sölle and Roberts provide responses to Marley's "redemption songs." Both Marley and Sölle contend that the place from which sin is recognized as sin must lie beyond sin; the pairing of sin and reconciliation gestures toward hope for liberation.

Chapter 3 begins with the pitfalls of the missionary church in the colonies and the acknowledgment that missionaries brought their culture with them and passed it off as universal. The missionaries struggled with questions of Christ and culture and presented in the colonies a Christ who was "above culture" and "against culture." Missionary theology was not invested in the liberation of oppressive structures that consigned the poor to lives of poverty and indignity. The missionary approach highlighted salvation without liberation and deliverance from sin, without transformation of the vicious circles of death expressed in racism, sexism, classism, and poverty. Hope broke through as oppressed persons both in the Caribbean and the United States began to read the Bible for themselves and discovered God's "preferential option for the poor." Much attention is given to the work of theologian Hyacinth Boothe, who affirms that the gospel of Christ needs to be set free from cultural entrapment. The gospel must announce that change is required in economics and in structures of oppression that blight the futures of God's children.

Chapter 4 focuses on a discussion among J. E. Fison, Dorothee Sölle, R. G. Beasley-Murray, Leander Keck, and Karl Barth. Beasley-Murray's claim that the doctrine of baptism is the key that unlocks the doctrines of Christ, the Holy Spirit, the church, and the Christian life functions as a thesis statement throughout this chapter. Sölle teases out the implication of the baptism of Jesus for a theory of solidarity, while Keck highlights baptism as pivotal for a theology of cross and resurrection in the letters of Saint Paul.

Chapter 5 examines the signal contributions of Jacquelyn Grant, Katie Cannon, Kelly Brown Douglas, and Delores Williams in the explication of the relationship between Black and womanist approaches to theology. Grant advocates a womanist Jesus. She points out that the church has used Jesus to keep women in their place and that both Jesus and Black women are in need of liberation. Jesus has been held captive to patriarchy, racism, and classism. Douglas affirms that while the race question has been helpful for Black women, they must also deal with the woman question. It would be an error for womanist thinking to relegate sexism and patriarchy to the White church. Cannon is emphatic that the church—the Black church—is in need of a theology of grace. Grace needs to be transformative, as God's gift of forgiveness and mercy is coupled with the human response of participation in acts of liberation.

Chapter 6 asserts that James Cone was not the founder of Black theology, since, prior to his advent on the world stage, there were theologians such as Howard Thurman, Mary McCloud Bethune, Henry McNeal Turner, Jarena Lee, and Martin Luther King Jr. However, Cone did give Black theology a place in the academy and was a leader in relating Black theology and the Third World. Cone was also clear that the Black church was the home of Black theology and was intentional in training theologians for the church and academy. Although Cone included White theologians in his articulation of Black theology, he was emphatic in pointing out the flaws of White theologians—central among them was their penchant to do theology as if Black people did not exist. In recent years he provided the most trenchant critique of racism in the church and society. This chapter concludes with central questions Cone advances for the future of Black theology: Is Black faith adequate as a tool of critical analysis? Is the Black church an agent of transformation?

Chapter 7 highlights the contribution of Sidney Mintz and Richard Price in their classic text, *The Birth of African-American Culture: An Anthropological Perspective.* In recalling the journey of African ancestors across the "Black Atlantic" as chattel for forced labor on plantations in the New World, Mintz and Price inform us that ancestors were not passive but found ways to connect. For example, being in the same cramped space in their journey across the Black Atlantic forged a bond among enslaved persons, who referred to each other as shipmates. Much attention is given to the contexts in which Black Atlantic traditions were forged and formed as Black people created New World religions as tools of resistance in the transformation of the world that sought to define them as nonpersons.

The trauma of Black suffering continues as the stories of George Floyd, Eric Garner, Sandra Bland, Michael Brown, and twelve-year-old Tamir Rice unfold. These persons, who, like Martin Luther King Jr., Mary Ellen Pleasant, and Malcolm X, sacrificed their lives, remind us that Black lives matter and that the ancestors hold us accountable to give worth and value to God's children.

This text is a sequel to my earlier book, *Plantation Church: How African American Religion Was Born in Caribbean Slavery.* While *Plantation Church* excavated the historical roots of Black religion in the Caribbean and United States, *Black Theology and Black Faith* seeks to tease out the emergence and development of God-talk primarily in the Caribbean. There will be, from time to time, attempts to forge a conversation with Black theology from the United States. This approach will raise intercultural and interregional questions, with implications for gender, race, and class in the understanding of Christian doctrine from a Black religious perspective.

# Faith and History

There was a vital connection between faith and history in Black people's attempt to transcend their situation in the New World, as enslaved persons. Indeed, a new faith was forged as Africa's children journeyed across the Black Atlantic as human cargo to work on plantations.

On arrival in the New World, Africans were sold and assigned the status of chattel. Throughout the regions, drumming, dancing, and indigenous religious practices that remembered Africa were often forbidden. In spite of such restrictions, Black faith survived, as Africans soon discovered that they held certain religious beliefs in common and maintained a lively curiosity concerning the religion of their oppressors. African people who were transported to plantations in the New World generally believed in a high God who was not involved in the daily affairs of their lives. Although believed to be the creator of the world, this high God lived outside the world, perhaps somewhere in the sky. His absence in the affairs of people was compensated for by secondary deities who mediated between him and people. African peoples who survived the Middle Passage believed in the worship of ancestor spirits.

In "The Creation of Afro-Caribbean Religions and Their Incorporation of Christian Elements," Bettina Schmidt points out that during the early years of slavery, enslaved Africans were able to create new religions by combining elements of their faith in their new environment. Although African customs and practices were forbidden, they were able to invest the content of African beliefs in the worship of Christian saints. "Hence, African slaves began to use Christian iconography, and symbols, in order to hide their [African] beliefs and practices. Under the shield of Catholic saints, African deities were able to survive the long period of oppression."[1] These traits are

1. Bettina E. Schmidt, "The Creation of Afro-Caribbean Religions and Their Incorporation of Christian Elements: A Critique against Syncretism," *Transformation* 23 (October 4, 2006): 238.

true of Black church practices on both sides of the Black Atlantic. "They are pivotal focal points for understanding African forms of logic and spirituality, especially, with regard to experiences, of fortune, and misfortune, well-being and disease, life and death. These features are present in the religious traditions of Haitian, Dominican, Louisianan Vodun as well as Cuban, Brazilian, Trinidadian, Puerto Rican, and U.S. Orisha communities."[2] It is clear that there was more than a reciprocal relationship between the gods of Africa and the saints enslaved people encountered in the New World. Something new happened, as enslaved persons used elements of the master's religion to help trigger and sustain the memory of Africa as a tool for their liberation. Many scholars consider it something of a mystery that Africa's children would turn to the religion of their oppressors and seek the favor of the gods of their oppressors in the search for survival and liberation. Much of this book seeks to answer this mystery and unveil the ways in which Africa's children, whether in the Caribbean or in the Americas, merged African and Christian worldviews in an explication of their faith.

The histories of African peoples in the United States and the Caribbean are intertwined through the experience of the Middle Passage and their subsequent suffering as chattel. However, the decisive experience was not the negative history of slavery but the emergence of a Black faith that withstood the encounter with racism and the humiliation they experienced in church and society as their very humanity was questioned and denied. This humiliation and rejection made Africans in the diaspora identify with Jesus, whom they understood to be rejected and crucified by his own people. As enslaved persons identified with the suffering and rejection of Jesus, they would sing: "They nail my Jesus down, They put on him a crown of thorns, O see my Jesus hangin' high! He look so pale an' bleed so free: O don't you think it was a shame, he hung three hours in dreadful pain?"[3]

Africa's children became victims of slavery, poverty, racism, and mass incarceration in the New World. The seeming death of the gods of Africa

2. Dianne M. Stewart, *Three Eyes for the Journey: African Dimensions of the Jamaican Religious Experience* (New York: Oxford University Press, 2005), 24.

3. James H. Cone, *The Spirituals and the Blues* (New York: Seabury, 1972), 53.

made them question their relationship to Africa and their understanding of faith and life. Unlike European questions pertaining to faith and reason, Africa's children highlighted faith and life. They embraced suffering and at the same time refused to make peace with the conditions of that suffering. Black faith sings, dances, suffers, and issues forth in transformation. This approach to faith is highlighted throughout this book, as faith is more than correct belief, orthodoxy. Faith includes the transformation of personal, social, and corporate dimensions of life. Black faith is invested in the liberation of Black lives and is insistent that Black lives matter. Black faith thinks, prays, sings, dances, and leads to praxis that is transformational.

# The Social Context of Black Theology

**B**ecause the formation of Black theology was made possible through the traffic of Africa's children across the "Black Atlantic," as enslaved persons, it is important to consider the origins, context, and development of their talk about God, the world, and humanity. It is widely agreed that Africans and people of African descent are never without their religion. They take their religion to the fields, to markets, to funerals, to their festivals, and religion shapes their rituals and beliefs. Africa's children, caught in an inescapable web of bondage and suffering in the New World, turned to religion as a mode of resistance, on the one hand, and as a means of protecting and preserving soul on the other hand. Questions of divine providence and theodicy were unavoidable. If Europeans came to the New World in search of freedom, it is clear that Africans came because of the loss of their freedom. Had their gods deserted them? How could Africans in the diaspora make theological sense of their existence in a strange land? How did enslaved Africans in the New World think about God, divine providence, and salvation, and how may we think about them?

If Black theology is understood as Black people agitating and engaging in struggle to change their world and construct God-talk in the process, it must be noted that Black theology's roots began in the Caribbean well over a hundred years prior to its emergence on the North American mainland. Enslaved Africans were brought to the Caribbean as early as 1501, according to Chancellor Eric Williams, and we are reminded that the first twenty Africans landed in James Town, Virginia, in 1619. A related point is that the historical priority of enslaved persons in the Caribbean raises a question for Black theology—what does it mean to do Black theology from the perspective of a Black majority? It is widely agreed that about eleven million Africans were brought to the New World as enslaved persons, of which only about 450,000 ended up in the United States. In fact, more than three times this number went to Haiti.

What does it mean to do Black theology from the perspective of a Black majority? And the converse is also relevant—what does it mean to do Black theology from the perspective of a Black minority? What does it mean for Black theology to acknowledge that the Black religious experience began in the Caribbean and not in the United States of America? The seeming death of the gods of Africa, perhaps in the Middle Passage, caused Africa's children, caught in the trauma of slavery, to begin to question their relationship to Africa and their understanding of faith and life. Unlike European questions pertaining to faith and reason, the questions of Africans during the holocaust of New World slavery made connections between faith and life. Central questions had to do with the meaning of suffering. Why does African peoples' suffering seem to be without end? It was in the context to make sense of their suffering that Jesus became a companion and friend.

> They nail my Jesus down,
> They put on him the crown of thorns,
> O see my Jesus hangin' high!
> He look so pale an' bleed so free:
> O don't you think it was a shame,
> He hung three hours in dreadful pain?[1]

The embrace of their suffering and at the same time a refusal to make peace with the conditions of that suffering was one reason why enslaved persons found strength in the cross of Jesus. Many enslaved persons felt that Jesus knew the way through the valley of suffering and that, as a friend, he would guide them through, and if Jesus did not act in a timely way to help them through the painful vale of suffering, appeal would be made to other spirits.

What Africans today call the "juju man," West Indians the "obeah man," and American Negroes the "hoodoo man" performed the function of al-

---

1. Quoted in James H. Cone, *The Spirituals and the Blues* (New York: Seabury, 1972), 53.

laying anxiety, assuring good luck, and confounding enemies. And some of them were believed to have the power of wreaking destruction upon a client's enemies. All such practitioners were defined as "agents of the devil" by Christians, and traffic with them as sin. New World Negroes continued to deal with them, however—or at least believe in their powers—even when they became Christians.[2]

## Black Theology and Race

James Cone has emerged as one of the founders of Black theology, and many of us who teach and write in the area of Black theology studied with Cone and continue to be in conversation with him, even beyond the grave. It is fitting that a Caribbean approach to theology would be in conversation, from time to time, with sisters and brothers in the United States. The truth is, we share a common history of oppression and a common goal of liberation. Further, the basic reality of our communal existence is poverty, which plagues the majority of Black folks, whether in the Caribbean or in the United States. A paradox for brothers and sisters in the United States who struggle with the reality of poverty is that they live in the midst of an economy of abundance, yet their unemployment rates are at least twice that of White people. Michelle Alexander, in her pathfinding text *The New Jim Crow*, problematizes the issue: "The United States now has the highest rate of incarceration in the world. . . . The racial dimension of mass incarceration is its most striking feature. No other country in the world imprisons so many of its racial or ethnic minorities. The United States imprisons a larger percentage of its black population than South Africa did at the height of apartheid. In Washington, D.C., our nation's capital, it is estimated that three out of four young black men (and nearly all those in the poorest neighborhoods) can expect to serve time in prison."[3]

2. St. Clair Drake, *The Redemption of Africa and Black Religion* (Chicago: Third World, 1970), 20.

3. Michelle Alexander, *The New Jim Crow: Mass Incarceration in the Age of Colorblindness* (New York: New Press, 2020), 6–7.

Alexander points out that people of all ethnicities use drugs at similar rates, and that White youth are more likely to engage in drug crimes than people of color. Yet jails in the United States bespeak a different reality, as jails are "overflowing with black and brown drug offenders. In some states, Black men have been admitted to prison on drug charges at rates twenty to fifty times greater than white men."[4] In some urban areas, as many as 80 percent of young African American men have criminal records that trigger many forms of discrimination—employment discrimination; housing discrimination; and lack of access to voting, educational opportunities, and other benefits.

Too many Black and Brown persons in the United States have become a part of a racial caste because of the color of their skin. A conclusion reached is that mass incarceration in the United States is about the social control of Black and Brown people. "The stark and sobering reality is that, for reasons largely unrelated to actual crime trends, the American penal system has emerged as a system of social control unparalleled in world history. And while the size of the system alone might suggest that it might touch the lives of most Americans, the primary targets of its control can be defined by race."[5] Black people in the United States compose a racial caste, "a stigmatized racial group locked into an inferior position by law and custom. Jim Crow and slavery were caste systems. So is our current system of mass incarceration."[6]

The analysis by Michelle Alexander indicates that Black theologians have not missed the mark in pointing out that the central theological problem facing people of color in the United States is racism. Racism is not merely the assertion of White privilege by the dominant race, Alexander says, but the bracketing of the humanity of Black and Brown peoples. Alexander's depiction of oppressed people being subjugated to a caste calls attention to a tragedy in which the bodies of Black and Brown persons once again belong to the master class, as was the case in New World slavery. The dilemma fac-

4. Alexander, *The New Jim Crow*, 7.
5. Alexander, *The New Jim Crow*, 8.
6. Alexander, *The New Jim Crow*, 12.

ing Black and Brown persons who are trapped in this caste system of mass incarceration reminds us that, at its peak, slavery in the United States did not exceed 450,000 persons, while the prison population of Black and Brown persons under mass incarceration is closer to 900,000. The root cause, according to Alexander, Cone, and other Black theologians, is racism.

The subjugation of Black and Brown persons threatens their humanity. James Cone offers an interpretation of the underlying pathology for Black and White people "turning on each other rather than turning to each other." The malady is fear and hate, with fear becoming the basis of hate. "Whites have a deep primordial and profound psychological fear of Blackness. . . . Blacks fear whites too. But the Black fear of White is often well grounded."[7] An aspect of the problem here is the power differential between Black and White persons, added to the notion that people usually hate what they fear. "Many white policemen kill unarmed black people—shooting teenagers in the back—because they hate and fear blackness. One-third of black men we are told, between the ages of 19–29 are involved in the legal system—i.e., in prison, on parole, or waiting for their case to come up in court. . . . Approximately one half of the two million people in America's prisons are black. If such percentages were found in the white community, . . . (America) would declare a national emergency."[8]

Questions of fear and power highlighted the conversation between Martin Luther King Jr. and students from the Student Nonviolent Coordinating Committee (SNCC) who contended that while they had love for persons who sought to destroy them, they lacked power to change their situation of powerlessness. They concluded that love without power was anemic; therefore, they started to chant the phrase "Black power," as power coupled with love could aid in the transformation of their situation. There is a real danger that the situation of mass incarceration in the United States coupled with the sense of powerlessness in the African American community requires that practices of reconciliation be coupled with love and power.

7. James H. Cone, "The Easy Conscience of America's Churches on Race," in *Spirituality and Justice*, ed. Bill Thompson (reprint, Chicago: CTA, 2003), 3.
8. Cone, "The Easy Conscience of America's Churches on Race," 3.

The youth leadership in the SNCC expressed the fear that they were confronted with a situation in which Black people had all the love, so to speak,
while White people had all the power. James Cone suggests that this is the
meaning of White supremacy, a situation in which White people control
the levers of power. "It is everywhere—controlling the centers of economic,
political, intellectual, and religious power. This is what white supremacy
means—white control of all resources essential for human wellbeing. . . .
White institutions seldom change because a few token people of color are
placed in high positions."[9]

Unlike in the United States, there is no overt racial discrimination throughout the Caribbean. There is no history of Jim Crow or lynching; schools,
restaurants, theaters, and public transportation are open to all people.

> Cases of rape of white women are unknown, and we have the testimony
> of an ex-governor of Jamaica [who was white] as to the safety of white
> women, anywhere at any time. White, brown, and black meet in the same
> churches in which pews, at a price, can be obtained by one and all. The
> graves of whites, browns, and blacks are seen side by side in cemeteries.
> The declaration of fundamental rights proclaimed by Cuba may be indic-
> ative of the legal situation in the Caribbean: "All Cubans are equal before
> the law. The Republic recognizes no privileges. All discrimination because
> of sex, race, color or class, or other affront to human dignity is declared
> illegal and punishable."[10]

Although these claims were made in the 1940s by Dr. Eric Williams, who
wrote then as a professor at Howard University, most are still true throughout the Caribbean. His analysis, however, did not take into account the
power differential and the history of race relations in reference to Black,

9. Cone, "The Easy Conscience of America's Churches on Race," 3.
10. Eric Williams, *The Negro in the Caribbean* (New York: Negro University Press, 1942),
62–63. Williams paints a picture of an egalitarian society. It is still difficult to find cases of
White women who are sexually assaulted by natives of the Caribbean. Unfortunately, this
is not always the case for Caribbean women.

Brown, and White relationships. Whites were always protected by the color of their skin and used religion, church, and the force of law to argue that God chose them to be protectors and masters over Black and Brown people in the Caribbean. Much of the ethos that characterizes relationships among racialized groups in the Caribbean is a spillover from the era of slavery.

New World slavery continued in Cuba until 1886, and several of my peers recall stories from their great-grandparents about proper etiquette and the master class. Life in the colonies even in the world painted by Eric Williams was not without the imbalance of power, relations of inequality, or domination in which persons considered White were often viewed as above the law and in total control and power in the wider society. The rest of us were everything but White. Dr. Williams, who became prime minister of Trinidad and Tobago, points to the different understandings of color throughout the Caribbean. "Haitians consider themselves 'blacks,' not Negroes. It is difficult, too, for the American Negro to realize that the term 'colored' signifies a distinct group in the Caribbean.... The English islands spoke of the 'people of color'; in the French they were 'gens de couleur'; in Spanish 'gente de color.' One is not a mulatto in Cuba or Puerto Rico—one might be 'pardo,' or 'moreno,' or 'trigueno,' indicating different shades of brown."[11] Williams's analysis of race relations in the Caribbean may help us understand why the civil rights movement led by Dr. King did not kindle the political imagination of Caribbean people and result in mass protest movements throughout the Caribbean.

In calling attention to the profound distinctions in race relations in the United States and the Caribbean, Williams points out that if one drop of "Negro" blood makes one a "Negro" in the United States, in Caribbean nations the shade of one's skin is the determining factor. While the question of one's relationship to White prestige may be important for the emergent middle class, this was not the case for the Black masses at the bottom of the racial and political pyramid. In the 1950s and 1960s, it was not unusual to see Black men who studied in American or European universities return home to the Caribbean with White wives. This provided instant access to the

11. Williams, *The Negro in the Caribbean*, 63.

middle class. It was often said that the next best thing to being White was to marry White. But this was not available to the Black underclass. "The middle class elite in the Caribbean is Christian or free-thinking, while the masses still cling to ancient beliefs and rites, as the 'voodoo' of Haiti, the 'Shango' of Trinidad, the 'pocomania' of Jamaica. . . . The main aim of the Caribbean colored middle class is to forget their African origin."[12] And yet it does not matter how hard the brokers of power try, the Black middle class, whether in the United States or in the Caribbean, cannot sever their history from the triangular relationship between Africa, the Caribbean, and the United States—a relationship rooted in the memory of Africa.

## Marcus Garvey and Black Theology

In many Caribbean nations, the overthrow of colonialism and the advent of political independence is an expression of Marcus Garvey's advocacy of democratic traditions that honor majority rule. Most Caribbean nations received political independence in the 1960s, except for Haiti, which had become a republic in 1804. Additionally, Garvey is regarded as the prophet of the Rastafari faith, and many elders of this faith attribute the founding of Rastafarianism to a comment by Garvey, who, on an occasion when leaving Jamaica for Harlem, New York, counseled the people of Jamaica: "Look to Africa from which a king will arise," a paraphrase of Psalm 68:31. Garvey has had profound impact on the political and religious development of Caribbean nations.

In an interview with the *Daily Gleaner, Jamaica*, Malcolm X was asked to comment on the influence of his mother on his thinking. Malcolm states:

> Most people in the Caribbean area, are still proud that they are black, proud of the African blood, and their heritage, and I think this type of pride was instilled in my mother, and she instilled it in us, too, to the best degree that she could. She had—despite the fact that her father was

12. Williams, *The Negro in the Caribbean*, 64.

white—more African leanings, and African pride, and a desire to be identified with Africa. In fact she was an active member of the Marcus Garvey movement. My father, besides being an active worker in the Marcus
Garvey movement, was a Christian clergyman—a Baptist minister. He
was lynched in Lansing, Michigan, 1954, by being thrown under a street
car. . . . Every time you see another nation on the African continent become independent, you know that Marcus Garvey is alive. It was Marcus
Garvey's philosophy of Pan Africanism that initiated the entire freedom
movement, which brought about the independence of African nations and
had it not been for Marcus Garvey, and the foundation laid by him, you
would find no independent nations in the Caribbean today. . . . All the
freedom movements that are taking place right here in America today are
initiated by the work and teachings of Marcus Garvey. The entire Black
Muslim philosophy here in America is feeding upon the seeds that were
planted by Marcus Garvey.[13]

Malcolm X could not escape the influence of Marcus Garvey, as both of
his parents were active in the movement that Garvey led. What Martin
Luther King Jr. was to the American South, Malcolm X was to the American North. The Great Migration of Black people from the South to the
North, which "began before the First World War and continued through
the 1950s, marked a significant change in the content and texture of their
lives. The contrast between what blacks expected to find in the 'promised
land' of the North and what they found was so great that frustration and
indignity ensued, destroying much of their self-esteem and pride. Blacks
expected to find the freedom which had eluded them for so many years in
the South. They expected to have the right, like other Americans, to live
wherever they chose and to work and play with whomever they chose."[14]
Yet their reality in this new space and place in the American North turned
out differently.

13. Amy Jacques Garvey, *Garvey and Garveyism* (New York: Macmillan, 1970), 306–7.
14. James H. Cone, *Martin and Malcolm and America: A Dream or a Nightmare* (Maryknoll, NY: Orbis Books, 1992), 90.

In several respects, the North turned out to be worse than the South, as Black people were crammed into urban centers and forced to pay exorbitant prices for rent, food, and other necessities. They were also harassed by white police, who showed them no respect. Black hopes were dashed as the "promised land" proved to be a mirage. Garvey, who had the headquarters of his Back to Africa Movement in Harlem, placed these issues in theological perspective and suggested that liberation has to be more than a word—it has to be a way of life. A Christian understanding of faith should not be all about tomorrow but must be empirically grounded in the here and now. It is not the Christian understanding of faith to postpone liberation for tomorrow or for an understanding of heaven that does not transform life in the present. Christian faith should announce that liberation from economic privations and social conditions that demean and diminish the human spirit is not merely a goal at the end of history but, through the exercise of faith informed by hope and love, is present in history. Garvey captures this sentiment:

> The people . . . want advanced religion now. The religion that will prepare them for heaven by having them live clean, healthy, happy and prosperous lives down here. No hungry man [person] can be a good Christian. No dirty, naked, civilized man [person] can be a good Christian. No shelterless civilized man [person] can be a good Christian for he is bound to have bad wicked thoughts, therefore, it should be the duty of religion to find physical as well as spiritual food for the body of man; so when you preachers ignore the economic condition and moral depravity of the people, they are but serving themselves through preaching and not representing the spirit of God.[15]

Garvey was an early Black theologian insisting that liberation had to be more than a word and that the gospel at its best had to address the needs of the total person. During the era of plantation slavery in the New World,

15. Amy Jacques Garvey, *Garvey and Garveyism*, 61.

it was understood by planters and missionaries that the bodies of enslaved persons belonged to the master and the souls belonged to God; heaven and earth, like soul and body, were separated. The Christian Scriptures make it clear that the core of the ministry of Jesus was liberation for all who were oppressed. "Using the lens of the African American experience, [Cone] argued that the core message of the Bible paradigmatically expressed by Jesus the Anointed One was liberation of the materially poor. Consequently, ecclesial formations, educational venues, and civic society were called by God to focus on the liberation of the least in society: the broken-hearted, the wounded, working people, the outcast, the marginalized, the oppressed, and those surviving in structural poverty."[16]

## Colonial Perspectives

Missionaries often had other ideas. The Caribbean has a long history of the Christian missionary plying his understanding of God and what it meant for the children of Africa to come within the pale of the church.

> The chief significance of the New World, in [Columbus's] eyes, was the opportunity it afforded of bringing multitudes into the Catholic faith. On his return from his first voyage, he ended his narrative of his exploits to the Sovereigns with the assurance that "God had reserved for the Spanish monarchs, not only all the treasures of the New World, but a still greater treasure of inestimable value, in the infinite number of souls destined to be brought over into the bosom of the Christian Church." . . . It has been said of the Spanish conquistadors that first they fell on their knees, and then they fell on the aborigines.[17]

16. See Dwight Hopkins, "General Introduction," in *The Cambridge Companion to Black Theology*, ed. Dwight Hopkins and Edward P. Antonio (Cambridge: Cambridge University Press 2012), 13.

17. Eric Williams, *From Columbus to Castro: The History of the Caribbean, 1492–1969* (New York: Vintage Books, 1969), 20, 30.

The colonial Caribbean was not at peace with promises from missionaries that Christianity would make enslaved persons submissive and subordinate. The problem, the master class argued, was, even if Christianity made enslaved persons more dutiful, what if these enslaved persons caught on to the liberating possibilities of freedom enshrined in the Christian Scriptures? Then the kindness of masters would not be enough; enslaved persons would press for freedom. It was at this level that the master class understood Christianity as a double-edged sword. On the one hand, Christianity may produce a dutiful servant, but on the other hand, it may give rise to one who yearned for freedom.

The immediate fear of the ruling class was that freedom would mean insubordination, revolts, and an understanding that subjugation was wrong and not in keeping with the Bible's teaching about God's will for Africa's children. It should not surprise us, then, that during much of the nineteenth century, throughout the Caribbean, Africa's children did not attend colonial churches, as they were not welcomed there. James Phillippo, the British missionary who spent twenty years in Jamaica, comments:

> Not only were they oppressed and bowed down by the operation of unjust and cruel laws, but there was yet another circumstance connected with the condition of the colored and black population, in some respects still more painful. The most inveterate prejudice existed against them on account of their color. Hence they were universally prohibited all intercourse of equality with whites, and if of such an opprobrious distinction they ventured to complain, they were often insultingly told that they were "the descendants of the ourand-outang," that their mothers hunted the tiger in the wilds of Africa; and that but for the generosity of their sires, in place of possessing freedom and property, their lot would have been to dig cane-holes beneath the discipline of the driver's whip. At church, if a man of color, however respectable in circumstance of character, entered the pew of the lowest white man, he was instantly ordered out. . . . With

people of color, indeed, the whites, like the Egyptians in reference to the Israelites, held it an abomination to eat bread.[18]

## God and the Black Experience

Racism was clearly slavery's original sin. What occurs in the subjugation of another human being, on the basis of race, is a failure to understand that in God's election of Jesus Christ (2 Cor. 4:4 and Col. 1:15), God has chosen all humanity as daughters and sons. The call to be members of the family of God provides equal access to the tree of life. The gospel declares that all human beings are made in the divine image. As was made clear in the ejection of Richard Allen and Absalom Jones from St. Georges Methodist Church in Philadelphia, Black people discovered that they preferred to worship among themselves and looked forward to their own preachers interpreting the Bible.

This connection between God-talk and the Black experience provided a basis for Black theology. "Since its origins in the 1960s, black theology of liberation has matured into a body of knowledge defined by its own origins, traditions, norms, global indigenous forms, and kindred disciplines. In this sense, black theology takes place wherever darker-skinned peoples in the world reflect on their faith and liberation within their own local contexts. . . . (One) commonality was the issue of race or the discrimination suffered by darker-skinned people in various countries."[19]

It becomes clear that from a Caribbean perspective colonial theology was not invested in the liberation of oppressed people. Colonial theology was an imported product that sought to impose a foreign experience on the victims of oppression. Colonial theology fostered a sense of dependence on the host country. I recall, from growing up in Jamaica, that the form

18. James M. Phillippo, *Jamaica: Its Past and Present State* (London: John Snow, 1843; reprint, Westport, CT: Negro University Press, 1970), 147–48.
19. Hopkins, "General Introduction," 14.

of worship in most mainline churches was imported, including hymnals, liturgies, and our understanding of God. There was a real danger that God was a foreigner, especially since much of the language in our prayers and devotion was not our local dialect "patwa" but the Queen's English, which most persons struggled to understand.

Recently, the New Testament was translated into the Jamaican language. It was a breakthrough for the Jamaican people, as it allowed us to hear the New Testament read in our own language. To have the Word of God in the language of the masses of people rather than in the language that is comfortable for the seminary-trained preacher was extraordinary, as it called into question the colonial strategy of domination. The New Testament can now be read not only in the language of the queen but also in the language of the masses. The Jamaican New Testament is a watershed moment for Jamaica because, for over three hundred years, we have regarded our history, our language, and ourselves as less-than, as inferior, and now, with the Word of God in our own tongue, we learn that God does not only understand us when we pray in our own language, "patwa," but God speaks to us in "patwa." God understands the nuances of our language and does not speak Jamaican with an accent. The persons in our culture who speak Jamaican with an accent are strangers; they are from elsewhere.

The Jamaican New Testament points to the divine humility as God embraces the Black experience and becomes one of us. Although we have been bilingual for some time, it did not dawn on our consciousness that God speaks our native tongue. In our dreams and vision God always appears speaking proper English, because this was how God was presented in our liturgies and in the reading of Scripture and in the preaching of the Word in church. Then, we felt that God did not appreciate or understand the indigenous culture. God was a stranger. God was among us as a foreigner.

However, we now know that there is no language that is inferior and should be excluded from being a bearer of the Word of God. God speaks through the Black experience and uses it as a bearer of the divine truth. Additionally, we are now clear that no one language is indispensable. The community at worship is now invited to engage God not only with the language of the head, but also with the language of the heart. The priority of the Black experience is supported by the Word of God in our own tongue.

## Voices from the Caribbean

Oscar La Croix, a parish priest from Guadeloupe, supported protecting Caribbean identity and culture from the encroachments of imperial and colonial influences handed down from the United States and Europe. Among the imported values Caribbean people should guard against are, he writes, "a general context of valorization of western patterns and of the white man, and a depreciation of the Blackman and all that is Indigenous; because everything was imported, a mentality of dependence and passivity, opposed to all creativity and initiative. A Gospel brought by . . . missionaries who apart from some fortunate exceptions, put forward their theological culture, language of the faith . . . a frequent policy of compromise between church authority and civil powers."[20]

Although Father La Croix writes from a French-speaking community in the Caribbean, his claims have currency throughout the region and address theological claims embraced by churches that were indoctrinated by European and North American missionaries. La Croix began an address to the Caribbean Conference of Churches by critiquing the valorization of Western ways of thinking and the assumed superiority of White people. According to La Croix, the penchant to defer to theological and ecclesial positions from Europe and the United States is a throwback to plantation slavery in the region, and this must give way to practices of reconciliation that open doors for the emergence of a new humanity in the Caribbean. La Croix implored the conference to conjoin mission and ministry as the church is reminded of its primary task of salvation. "The Church is not at the service of herself, but of the Gospel; she holds her mission from Jesus Christ; in other

20. Oscar La Croix, "How the Church Conceives of Her Mission in the French West Indies," in *Out of the Depths*, ed. Idris Hamid (San Fernando, Trinidad: Rahaman Printery, 1977), 232. Hereafter, page references from this work will be given in parentheses in the text.

words, her mission is based upon Holy Scriptures, which has already begun to be lived and realized in history (hence, the importance of Tradition), with errors and hesitations, and continues to be thought, studied, proposed in official documents (like those of Vatican II and those of the World Council of Churches)" (231).

The point of departure for talk about the emergence of a new humanity in the Caribbean must be Jesus Christ. According to La Croix, the church must speak with specificity to people in the Caribbean in the light of the real conditions and needs that confront them in the real situation in which they live. Black theology in the Caribbean must not talk about people in general but must address the real needs of people in the context of faith and life. La Croix focused the issue for us:

> It is fitting that the salvation announced and inaugurated by Christ, Lord and Savior be understood and lived as a total liberation of the Caribbean man [person]. Because of our foreign heritage of ideas, our faith has too often been a private affair, confined to certain domains of our existence. To be faithful to Christ, the church must be able to live and announce salvation in all dimensions, giving special attention to its collective aspects. . . . The signs that the Spirit of God has already brought about salvation and His Kingdom are certainly patience, meekness and goodness . . . but also the struggle against prevailing and institutionalized injustices. (234)

La Croix encouraged the conference to guard against the gap between faith and life. The theological task is to mediate between the faith enshrined in the tradition and Scripture and the real world in which people struggle against institutional forms of injustice, racism, and materiality. Faith must take shape in the Caribbean as Black theology announces and points to the Christ who liberates real people in the real world.

The Caribbean church is called to point to the Christ who liberates and calls people to salvation. "If the church wants to be the universal sign of universal salvation, it cannot ignore any of the great problems which occupy the mind of the Caribbean man [person] of to-day: unemployment, emigration, economic and cultural pressures, the reality of the Caribbean family (matrifocality and 'machismo' for instance). All this reality is the fabric of salvation" (235). La Croix highlighted several loci for a Black theology in the Caribbean. The church must be mission oriented as it takes on the form of Christ in history and in the world. It is Jesus the Christ as Savior who restores the damaged identity of Caribbean people as he points them to a new humanity and identity. Sources of this incipient theology are Scripture, history, tradition, and the magisterium.

Doctrines that need to be proclaimed in the midst of the world, and in church, are Christology, the Trinity, revelation, salvation, providence, and theodicy. "Furthermore, the Church must aim at incarnating the Gospel and at giving it an indigenous expression. On that point much progress remains to be done otherwise the Gospel will be looked upon as a produce of importation. . . . Our churches and their liturgical equipment are too much copied on western patterns. . . . What matters is to set into motion the dynamics of liberation" (237).

While La Croix, who represented the French islands of Martinique and Guadeloupe at the conference, emphasized the need for "decolonizing theology," Uxmal Livio Diaz, a Christian pastor from Cuba, argued for going beyond decolonizing theology and building a Black liberation theology in the Caribbean. He put it this way in his address: "We talk a lot in the Caribbean about the decolonization of theology, and I think that is good, but so far what I've read speaks of a negative theology set over against the one Colonialism brought us; since theology is above all an affirmation, 'God's yes,' we must go a little further and opt for a 'Black Liberation Theology' in which we make explicit and tie together all the feeling of all those who are racially and economically exploited in the Caribbean, and which will offer us the possibility of a liberating praxis for the people of God."[21] Diaz helps us see the limits of a decolonizing theology and acknowledges that it is a first step toward the liberation of theology, which should aid us on the journey to

---

21. Uxmal Livio Diaz, "The Role of Third World Christians and Churches in the Struggle against Colonialism and NeoColonialism," in Hamid, *Out of the Depths*, 142.

liberation from the sin that besets us personally and in the social structures of society. The insight to move beyond a critique of colonialism and begin to embrace our own liberation is of first importance. How do Caribbean nations engage in nation building? What are appropriate models of a just society in which there are equity, fairness, and possibilities for the emergence of a new humanity in the Caribbean?

It seems that Diaz sees decolonization as a first step, and the overarching concern is that the vision of the new humanity is kept in mind. "This process of colonization also imposed on the Caribbean, more than on the rest of America, our commercial and production patterns; that is, our peoples traditionally have produced not for their own benefit but for that of the colonizer; and by production I mean not only minerals, agriculture, livestock, semi-manufactured goods, etc., *but even our thought.* Thus, we have passed through a process of being robbed of our identity, to identify ourselves with the colonizers, in their values, customs, languages, religious thought."[22] Diaz here does the hard work of decolonizing Caribbean culture and reminds Caribbean people that too much of our production is for the colonizer and not for ourselves.

One of the planks of a Black liberation theology that addresses the need for the emergence of a new humanity in the Caribbean is the need to spend less time with the colonizer and more time with the colonized, less time with the oppressor and more with the oppressed. The first principle is that of Black awareness, the need for people of African descent to know their history, their culture, and their heritage. An appropriate starting point is "Black people, know yourselves." Knowledge of self includes both sociological and educational tasks. The sociological tasks include assessment of Black institutions; the means of production, including ownership of land; and the place of the marginalized in the economic order.[23] The principle of Black awareness has been invaluable for the journey toward political independence throughout

22. Diaz, "The Role of Third World Christians," 133.
23. Marcus Garvey Jr., "Garveyism: Some Reflections on Its Significance for Today," in *Marcus Garvey and the Vision of Africa*, ed. John Henrik Clarke with the assistance of Amy Jacques Garvey (Baltimore: Black Classic, 1974), 375.

the Caribbean, as awareness includes the notion of being awakened to one's circumstance and identity. To be aware and awakened means that one is able and ready to engage action informed by reflection on one's history and culture, to forge a new direction with determination to effect change. A crucial aspect of this awareness of one's world and identity is the knowledge of self-world. For Marcus Garvey, it was of first importance that as people of African descent restore the image of the self that was stolen during slavery, they recall and remember their heritage. A central question Garvey addressed to people of African descent may be paraphrased: Where do you stand in relation to Africa? The principle of Black awareness and awakening is integrally related to this question for Garvey.

Black awareness and Black awakening have to do with Black people's encounter with spirit. The gift of divine spirit increases awareness of one's social location and one's world. To be "grasped by spirit" increases awareness and enhances the gift of awakening as one becomes keenly aware of the demonic within one's actual situation, including the forces against which one must struggle in the quest to restore the broken self.[24] Black awareness and Black awakening lead one on the path to increasing freedom and open one to new possibilities of liberation and emancipation.

Bob Marley, in his *Exodus* album, captures the spirit of freedom inspired by Black awareness and Black awakening. "We know where we're going. We know where we're from. We're leaving Babylon. We're going to our Father's land. Exodus. Movement of Jah people."[25]

The first principle of Black awareness, which for Garvey really meant African awareness, would not have been embraced by Dr. King throughout most of his life. King had philosophical and theological problems with essentializing the Black experience. Throughout most of the years of King's

24. See Paul Tillich, *Systematic Theology*, vol. 3 (Chicago: University of Chicago Press, 1967). Tillich's discussion of principles determining the New Being as process is very helpful at this point.

25. Bob Marley and the Wailers, *Exodus* (Island Records, 1977), Stereo IS-089-A. See *The Complete Lyrics of Bob Marley: Songs of Freedom*, ed. Harry Hawke (London: Omnibus, 2001), 48–49.

leadership of the civil rights movement, his goal was not Black community. He believed that such a focus could pose a problem and be understood as a way to keep segregation in the Black community in place. To advocate the replacement of White community with Black community would be interpreted as a reversal of values, the replacement of White supremacy with Black power. Unlike Marcus Garvey, King did not press for Black nationalism but instead pressed for a new reality beyond black and white that at the same time included both. This new reality King called "the Beloved Community." "We must all learn to live together as brothers [and sisters], or we will perish as fools. We are tied together in a single garment of destiny, caught in an inescapable network of mutuality. And whatever affects one directly affects all indirectly—This is the way God's universe is made; this is the way it is structured."[26]

## King and Garvey

If the early King articulated an easy optimism that pointed in the direction of a community in which the sacredness of each person is respected, he had not yet, like Garvey, asked about African consciousness or African awakening as a way of dealing with the issues of power and justice that are integral to authentic community. Throughout the Caribbean, there was an understanding of power influenced by Garvey and fired by the question, "Where do you stand in relation to Africa?" which resulted in the articulation and embrace of "Black power." While King had problems with the term "Black power," he seemed to accept the concept. "The plantation and the ghetto were created by those who had power, both to confine those who had no power and to perpetuate their powerlessness. The problem of transforming the ghetto, therefore, is a problem of power confrontation of the forces of power demanding change and the forces of power dedicated to preserving

26. Martin Luther King Jr., "Remaining Awake through a Great Revolution," in *Testament of Hope: The Essential Writings of Martin Luther King Jr.*, ed. James Melvin Washington, 3rd ed. (San Francisco: Harper & Row, 1986), 269.

the status quo. Now power properly understood is nothing but the ability to achieve purpose. It is the strength required to bring about social, political and economic change."[27]

Although the concepts of power seem to function in similar ways for King and Garvey, Garvey would make conceptual moves that King would not entertain. For Garvey, the notion of race pride was an indispensable aspect of power for Black people. Garvey lived in a world and time when whiteness as an ideal was elevated and blackness was despised by White people, and often Black persons as well. In Garvey's world, to be born White was to be socially privileged—to be born Black was to be marginalized. Inequalities in economic and racial terms made many Black people dissatisfied and displeased with the Black condition. It was in this context that Black people should view their world, including God, through an African lens. Garvey was completely against miscegenation, as he believed this was a way to destroy the Black race.

> Take down the pictures of white women from your walls. Elevate your own women to that place of honor. They are for the most part the burden-bearers of the race. Mothers! Give your children dolls that look like them to play with and to cuddle. They will learn as they grow older to love and to care for their own children and not neglect them. Men and women, God made us as his perfect creation. [God] made no mistake when he made us black with kinky hair. It was divine purpose for us to live in our natural habitat—the tropical zones of the earth. Forget the white man's banter that he made us in the night and forgot to paint us. That we were brought here against our will is just a natural process of the strong enslaving the weak. We have outgrown slavery, but our minds are still enslaved to the thinking of the master race. Now take these kinks out of your mind instead of out of your hair.[28]

27. Martin Luther King Jr., "Where Do We Go from Here?" in Washington, *Testament of Hope*, 246.
28. Cited by Marcus Garvey, in "Garveyism," 377.

In this marvelous passage Garvey highlights the body as a site for liberation. It is the body that represents the divine image. It was the body that was baptized; it was the body of Jesus that was sacrificed on the cross.

> Oh, dey whupped him up de hill, up de hill, up de hill,
> Oh, dey whupped him up de hill, an' he never said
> a mumbalin' word
> Oh, dey whupped him up de hill, an' he never said
> A mumbalin' word,
> He jes' hung down his head an' he cried.[29]

Garvey understood the importance of Black symbolism in building authentic Black community. Garvey would remind Black people that God, who is perfect, created them perfectly, with beautiful noses, lips, and woolly hair. Additionally, he would hand out Black dolls to parents in the Black community, as he claimed this would help young mothers love their children.

Much work needs to be done on the possible impact of Marcus Garvey on the teachings and life of Dr. King. Throughout most of his life, King was committed to the building of an integrated society, yet toward the end of his life he began to sound more like Garvey, calling on Black communities to support Black institutions. After 1966, King began to take a fresh look at his dream for America and concluded with Malcolm X that the likelihood of the dream morphing into a nightmare was a real possibility. Like Garvey and Malcolm, King began to learn of the intransigence of racism, and as his "Letter from a Birmingham Jail" made clear, he had lost confidence in the willingness of the white middle class to help turn back the tide of racism. Like Garvey, King began to instruct Black people to become self-reliant and proactive in developing their own businesses.

According to King, Black people should be willing to withdraw economic support from Coca-Cola, Sealtest milk, Wonder Bread, companies that King

---

29. Cone, *The Spirituals and the Blues*, 52.

observed were not invested in treating all God's children fairly.[30] However, although King began to sound like Garvey, he had not given up on his grand vision of the Beloved Community as the goal of the movement he led, and as a destination for the Black community. But there was a problem. King did not anticipate the stubborn refusal and resistance of the dominant culture to allow Black bodies to be present in schools, churches, restaurants, public transportation, and hospitals. King was clear that the American way of life was not consonant with the imperatives of the Christian gospel. The inclusive community was not just a question of social ethics; it was required by the gospel of Christ.

However, in spite of the quest for integration, King seems to argue for a modified form of segregation by counseling Black people to place their money in banks owned by Black people, and not to patronize companies that were not pro-Black. "We've got to strengthen black institutions. I call upon you to take your money out of the banks downtown and deposit your money in TriState bank—we want a 'bank-in' movement in Memphis. . . . You have six or seven black insurance companies in Memphis. Take out your insurance there."[31]

Coupled with this was the reality that he never counseled Black churches to integrate. Black churches have been segregated, both culturally and economically. Black churches have been one of the few Black institutions that are Black owned. Historically, this has been one of the few places where Black bodies have been free to study, teach, dance, pray, learn, and worship.

Also, King, like his parents, attended segregated colleges. As King began to embrace blackness, did he imply that perhaps there is a place for segregated schools, if they were the only rhetorical space where Black people were free to engage Black consciousness? Could it be that in 1968, the year King was assassinated, he had come to see that although the Beloved Community had emerged as the grand vision of the civil rights movement, because of the depth of the racist worldview that informed and dominated America, a limited

30. Martin Luther King Jr., "I See the Promised Land," in Washington, *Testament of Hope*, 283.

31. King, "I See the Promised Land," 283.

form of segregation was an emergency solution? King states clearly: "It is an unhappy truth that racism is a way of life for the vast majority of white Americans, spoken or unspoken, acknowledged and denied, subtle and sometimes not so subtle—the disease of racism permeates and poisons the whole body politic. And I can see nothing more urgent than for America to work urgently and passionately and unrelentingly—to get rid of the disease of racism."[32] Garvey anticipated King: "No Negro, let him be American, European, West Indian or African, shall be truly respected until the race as a whole has emancipated itself, through self-achievement and progress, from universal prejudice. The Negro will have to build his own government, industry, art, science, literature, culture, before the world will stop to consider him. . . . The race needs workers at this time, not plagiarists, copyists and mere imitators, but men and women who are able to create, to originate and improve, and thus make an independent racial contribution to the world and civilization."[33]

Bob Marley echoes Garvey as he reminds us that liberation is much more than the removal of physical chains. What is at stake is liberation from mental slavery and passivity. In the album *Uprising*, he urges his listeners to emancipate themselves from mental slavery and free their minds to sing "redemption songs."

> Won't you help to sing. These songs of freedom?
> Cause all I ever had. Redemption Songs.[34]

Marley was instructive. "Redemption songs" are expressions of God's grace and provide aid on the journey to emancipation. Writes Rex Nettleford, "This brings to mind the injunction of Marcus Garvey, in a speech he delivered in Menelik Hall, Nova Scotia, in 1937, when he called on Black people to emancipate themselves from mental slavery, this being a major responsibility for themselves and themselves alone. This exhortation was

---

32. King, "Remaining Awake," 270.

33. Amy Jacques Garvey, *Garvey and Garveyism*, 23.

34. Bob Marley and the Wailers, *Uprising* (Tuff Gong/Island, 1980). Performed by Bob Marley at Crystal Palace, London. See *Complete Lyrics of Bob Marley*, 119–20.

later echoed by the Rastafarian reggae superstar Bob Marley, in what has become a much sung and oft-repeated couplet."[35]

Garvey was often the unseen hand that shaped liberation and emancipation worldviews throughout the Caribbean and United States. In 1965 King was invited to address students at the University of the West Indies, in Jamaica, the birth home of Garvey. At a reception held in King's honor at the National Stadium, in which he received keys to the capital city of Kingston, King said, "In light of the many unpleasant and humiliating experiences with which I have to live, I am glad to feel like somebody in Jamaica. I really feel like a human being."[36] Later that day King laid a wreath at Garvey's shrine, an event attended by over two thousand persons. King spoke of the ways in which Garvey's life and mission informed his own work for civil and human rights in the United States:

> Marcus Garvey was the first man of color in the history of the United States to lead and develop a mass movement. He was the first man, on a mass scale, and level, to give millions of Negroes a sense of dignity and destiny, and make the Negro feel that he was somebody. You gave Marcus Garvey to the United States of America, and he gave to the millions of Negroes in the United States a sense of personhood, a sense of manhood, and a sense of somebodiness. As we stand here let us pledge ourselves to continue the struggle in this same spirit of somebodiness . . . in the conviction that all God's children are significant . . . that God's black children are just as significant as His white children. And we will not stop until we have freedom in all its dimensions.[37]

I recall how moving for Jamaicans it was to hear Martin Luther King Jr. say that he felt like a human being in Jamaica, implying that he did not al-

---

35. Rex Nettleford, "Discourse on Rastafari Reality," in *Chanting Down Babylon*, ed. Nathaniel Samuel Murrell, William David Spencer, and Adrian Anthony McFarlane (Philadelphia: Temple University Press, 1998), 313.

36. Amy Jacques Garvey, *Garvey and Garveyism*, 308.

37. Amy Jacques Garvey, *Garvey and Garveyism*, 308.

ways feel like somebody in the United States. Was it because he experienced what it felt like to be a part of a Black majority, not having to be preoccupied with issues of racial inequality and the erasure of Jim Crow laws that circumscribed the lives of the Black populace? There was in Jamaica and throughout the Caribbean an understanding that because we are a people who embrace an African ethos in music, art, religion, and lifestyle, we do not need to expunge the white bias in our society at the same level as our Black brothers and sisters in the United States. After all, Caribbean peoples felt that we had our civil rights movement in the 1920s through the teachings and advocacy of Garvey. Then we could live life on our terms because we were a part of a Black majority, and if change were to come, it would come from Africa, as Garvey and the Rastas prophesied, and not from the United States of America.

### Garvey and Rastafarianism

The story of Black theology in the Caribbean as the praxis of Black people agitating and protesting for equal rights and the right to choose their political destinies is incomplete without the contribution of the Rastafari faith. Since the 1930s, Rastas have believed that the emperor of Ethiopia, Haile Selassie, was God himself returned to deliver Black people from the scourge of oppression caused by colonialism and racism. The coronation of Haile Selassie in 1930 caused a great stir in Jamaica, and many people began to study their Bibles in an attempt to make theological connection between this strange happening in Ethiopia and the destitution and deep poverty of the masses of people in Jamaica. Rastafarianism was born out of the pain of oppression. There were long lines of people trying to buy bread, and the colonial government was insensitive to the needs of the masses of people. The coronation of a king in Ethiopia conjoined with a fabled comment by Garvey, "Look to Africa where a Black King shall arise—this will be the day of your deliverance." This prophecy by Garvey is a part of the oral tradition of Rastas and provided a new impetus for them to study their Bibles. Rastas are emphatic that they are not Christians, although they use the Christians' book and sing their songs.

By 1933 Rastas had begun to teach that their new king, Ras Tafari, was God, the "King of Kings" and the "Root of David." The main biblical focus for the new faith came from Revelation 5:2-5: "And I saw a mighty angel proclaiming with a loud voice, 'Who is worthy to open the scroll and break its seals?' And no one in heaven or on earth or under the earth was able to open the scroll or to look into it. . . . Then one of the elders said to me, 'Do not weep. See, the Lion of the tribe of Judah, the Root of David, has conquered, so that he can open the scroll and its seven seals'" (NRSV).[38] However, the Bible is not the authoritative source of truth for Rastas. The authoritative source of truth is "Jah" (Rastafari's word for God), as Jah reveals Jah's ways in national or world events or through the Bible. Jah's activities are not limited to the Bible, and Rastas often turn to the Bible for clues as to what Jah is up to in the world. Because of this, Rastas are busy exegeting the sociological and biblical texts. They often begin with the sociological text and then move to the biblical text for elucidation and affirmation of what Jah may be up to in the world.

This seems to be what happened in the 1930s with the founding of the Jah movement of Rastafari. According to Leonard Barrett, one of the pioneers of the study of Rastafari faith:

> The decade beginning in 1930 may well be called the "decade of despair" for the average Jamaican. The political situation was stagnant. The country was still in the hands of men who had little or no feeling for the hungry masses. . . . These were the years of the Great Depression, which saw lines of hungry people. . . . Most scholars agree that the movement originated soon after the coronation of Haile Selassie in Ethiopia. The coronation of this African king caused some Jamaicans of African descent both on the island and in New York to study their Bibles more closely. They remem-

---

38. Unless otherwise indicated, all Scripture references come from the New Revised Standard Version.

bered a pronouncement by Marcus Garvey: "Look to Africa where a Black King shall arise—this will be the day of your deliverance."[39]

As Rastas looked to the Bible and at what was happening in Africa, it was clear to them that the redemption of Black people was imminent through their new messiah, Haile Selassie. The twin concepts of the divinity of Haile Selassie and the redemption of Black people have distinguished Rastafari from other Afro-Caribbean movements that have sought to promote an awareness and awakening of Black consciousness in the Caribbean. Discourse concerning the divinity of Haile Selassie I and biblical warrants to justify this claim are made in the sociopolitical context in which Rastas as a community are at the base of the social and economic ladder.

But not only is the Bible being read in a social setting in which inequalities are rife and Rastafari as a community are despised, but it is also being read in a culture in which many Jamaicans and Caribbean people value those with lighter complexions more highly than their darker compatriots. Therefore, in this setting in which Rastas were devalued socially, economically, and racially, to proffer an image of God as a Rasta was a meaningful way to redeem and restore the tarnished image of Black people from indignity and disrespect.

The Rasta empress, Barbara Makeda Blake Hannah, in her consequential book *Rastafari: The New Creation*, calls attention to a basic tenet of Rastafari:

> The worship of Selassie I as the returned Messiah is held as a basic tenet of Rastafari faith. Though information about Selassie's life shows that he was a man with human weakness and faults, it is not unrealistic to perceive HIM (His Imperial Majesty) as Christ reborn, especially because of how racially

39. Leonard E. Barrett, *Soul-Force: African Heritage in Afro-American Religion* (New York: Anchor Press, 1974), 157–58.

liberating it has been for Black people to focus on a Black Christ-figure. When placed alongside the Prophet of Black Liberation—Marcus Garvey—the importance of Selassie I's life and logic of the Children of Africa in Jamaica recognizing the spiritual connection between HIM and themselves becomes clear. Even if the question of his divinity remains unverified until Kingdom come, it must be acknowledged that by his inspiration and in his name, Black brothers and sisters awakened and established a new and unique interest in God and Christ.[40]

Empress Hannah opens up for us new ways of understanding divinity and what it means for Rastas to become people of God. To be divine does not mean to be without sin or to be perfect, according to Empress Hannah. The divine shares his image with us and awakens us to Black liberation through inspiration and the power and majesty of his name. An interpretive key here is that the returned messiah is human and has become the Black Christ-figure, and it is his blackness that ensures our inspiration and liberation. This means that blackness is no longer a curse or a source of alienation but the means of liberation. The returned messiah enters into solidarity with the oppressed children of Africa and points them to God, who is Christ.

The way forward is clear. Rastas are emphatic that the European Christ is unsuitable to point the way out of the trap of poverty created for them by colonialism and the loss of identity facilitated by racist worldviews. Rastas' central contribution to the construction of a new humanity among Africa's children is that divine humility manifest in community as Christ, who is Black, joins the oppressed in solidarity and, through inspiration and the power and majesty of his name, baptizes them into the image of blackness in which they are made. In baptism of blackness, the oppressed die to whiteness and to colonial worldviews that institutionalize racism and master-slave

40. Barbara Makeda Blake Hannah, *Rastafari: The New Creation*, 4th ed. (Kingston, Jamaica: Masquel, 1997), 34–35.

relationships. Rastas become new architects and artisans of a new humanity in which the children of Africa are awakened to spiritual connections between themselves and their messiah, Haile Selassie I, in the formation of a new humanity.

It is reasonable to agree with Rastafari that the Europeanized Christ is unable to guide the community to liberation and salvation in a context in which the Black self has been damaged and in need of being restored. We learned from Marcus Garvey and Empress Hannah that the divine participates in our situation and empowers the victims of oppression to agitate and look for the revelation of the divine in their situation. It was this understanding among Black people in the Caribbean that allowed them to reject an either-or methodology and instead be open to a both-and approach to liberation and reconciliation. It was this approach to faith and life that made it possible for those brought to the New World as enslaved persons to consider the religion of their oppressors as a possible source of liberation. They would ask, what if elements of liberation are available in the good book the Bible? What if God speaks through this book, in spite of oppressors, who handle this book with dirty hands?

With this both-and approach to religion, they considered tenets of the master's religion and coupled them with their own African approach. This was one reason why oppressed persons throughout the Caribbean could belong to churches built and administered by the master class and at the same time build their own churches. This perhaps explains in part why, when I attended an African Orthodox church in Kingston, Jamaica, Rastas were in attendance waiting for a sprinkling of holy water that the priest threw in their direction after the baptism of babies. Perhaps that door was opened when it was reported that Haile Selassie I, in 1966, in a visit to Jamaica, told the Rasta community that he was Christian and they would find acceptance in the African Orthodox Church. But Rastas are clear that the Christian church is too closely associated with religion, and they are more in tune with worship and spirituality as a way of life.

However, the door is opened for communities that are different to come together, to struggle against the forces that seek to destroy their humanity. It is this coming together, to pray, to worship, to agitate, to struggle against the forces that tear the self apart, that provides the first planks of a theology of solidarity. It is in this sense that Black theology is in the service of oppressed communities, as the worship of God becomes the center of a great "welcome table" where diversity does not mean exclusion but means inclusivity and serves as a badge that affirms the humanity of all of God's children.

# CHAPTER 2

# Sin and Reconciliation

One of the themes we have struck in this text is the contextual nature of Black theology. If theology is the relating of the gospel of Christ to the historical and existential situation in which people "live and have their being," then the historical and cultural situation in which people live their lives is of first importance. The Christian story indicates that God came to human beings not in abstract and abstruse forms but concretely in his Son Jesus Christ. Christian faith highlights the concrete historical faith that signaled God's call to the children of Israel and God's presence among us in God's Son Jesus Christ.

The corollary is also true. If the gospel of grace came to us in a historical and contextual situation, sin also encounters us in the contexts and structures in which we live. Sin and grace do go together in Christian faith, and this provides one reason why in this chapter we will look at sin and its gesture toward life—reconciliation. It is of interest that, in the epistle to the church at Corinth, Paul admonishes Christians that "in Christ God was reconciling the world to himself" (2 Cor. 5:19).

## Stating the Problem

Often we are reminded that slavery is America's original sin. New World slavery is foundational to the American experience. The truth is that in the history of Black-White relations in the United States in particular, and in the New World in general, the fate of Black lives, from their capture in Africa to loading them on ships to cross the Middle Passage for sale in the New World, was determined by a trade in human flesh that constituted a sin against God and humanity. The sin of slavery ruptured the relationship of enslaved people with themselves, giving them a false identity as chattel and property as they were required to produce wealth to enrich the enslaver class. The sin of slavery at the initial level forced the enslaved to cultivate a divided self that perpetuated sin against self. The context of slavery sought to destroy the spirit of enslaved persons and, in the language of Martin Luther King Jr., "thingify the self." Slavery sought to reduce the human to the status of non-human. Paul captures this sentiment: "For what I would I do not, but what I hate, that I do (Romans 7.14)."[1] The sin of slavery was the rupture of ancestors from themselves, their families, their land, their religions, and their way of life. The Bible teaches that sin is not an isolated act that we are able to bracket and then move on from. Rather, like a ubiquitous virus, it has infected and affected the human family—including our institutions, the American Constitution, and our culture, engendering greed that birthed capitalism, which is a source of social and economic injustice. Anglo-Americans missed the truth concerning human beings when they encountered Africans and First Americans in the New World—that human beings were created for justice and love, and that our way of life in the world should be governed by an ethic of justice and care rather than an ethic of alienation. Scripture reminds us that "the wages of sin is death" (Rom. 6:23). An important aspect of the original sin of slavery was the failure of the enslaver to do justice and practice kindness to Africa's children (Mic. 6:8). Edward Baptist, in his important book *The Half Has Never Been Told*, illustrates the pernicious and death-dealing capacities of New World slavery:

> Between the arrival of the first Africans in 1619 and the outbreak of revolution in 1775, slavery had been one of the engines of colonial economic growth. The number of Africans brought to Maryland and Virginia before the late 1660s was a trickle—a few dozen per year. But along with white indentured servants, these enslaved Africans built a massive tobacco-production complex along the Chesapeake Bay and its tributaries. Over those formative fifty years, settlers imported concepts of racialized slavery from other colonies (such as those in the Caribbean, where enslaved Afri-

---

1. Dorothee Sölle, *Thinking about God: An Introduction to Theology* (Harrisburg, PA: Trinity Press International, 1990), 62. Sölle makes the point that sin alienates us from ourselves and destroys us.

cans already outnumbered other inhabitants by mid-seventeenth century). By 1670, custom and law insisted that children were slaves if their mothers were slaves, that enslaved Africans were to be treated as rights-less, perpetual outsiders (even if they converted to Christianity), that they should be whipped to labor, and that they could be sold and moved. They were chattel property. And everyone of visible African descent was assumed to be a slave.[2]

According to Baptist, for the first fifty years in the development of the colony of Virginia, Black and White persons worked together as indentured servants. Both Black and White persons were treated as less than fully human. After 1670, "by custom and law," White indentured labor was phased out and Blacks, because of the color of their skin, received an identity of slaves for life. The status of the Black woman (mother) defined the identity of her children. If the mother was a slave, the child was born a slave and could be whipped to labor. The enslaved were without rights, perpetual outsiders whose identity as Christians did not affect their status. One of the problems was that the church taught that enslaved persons were to render service to the enslaver as unto the Lord. It is rather sad that the church was complicit in keeping the Black person in a space and place prescribed by the system of slavery. By staying in their place, Black persons were subordinate and subservient to the ruling class. The Christian church knowingly participated in the culture of slavery, as when the Society for the Propagation of the Gospel owned a plantation in Barbados, in the Caribbean, and depended on slave labor. The same charge may be placed at the feet of George Whitefield, who depended on slave labor to run the orphanage that was essential to his ministry in South Carolina.

In these settings children of White servants were born free and the progeny of Black persons were born slaves. The Black child was owned by the enslaver even in her mother's womb. It was one of the travesties of the

2. Edward Baptist, *The Half Has Never Been Told: Slavery and the Making of American Capitalism* (New York: Basic Books, 2014), 3.

45

enslaved condition that enslaved persons had to honor the name of the enslaver/oppressor and were thereby unable to honor the name of their parents and ancestors. The enslaver had inordinate power over the enslaved persons—power often supported by the state and police force. Often the enslaver branded the enslaved on the cheek as a display of ownership. Enslaved persons were forbidden to use their African names and were forced to assume names assigned by the enslaver, often the master's name. These sins were to perpetuate the lie that the African was a person without a past.

In her essay "The Legacy of Slavery in New Orleans," Imani Perry points to sites of human trafficking in New Orleans. According to Perry, such sites are often difficult to identify in other US cities, but in New Orleans they cannot be avoided. "There were auction blocks in parks and sometimes aboard docked ships. A Black person suited for labor—skilled or manual, childbearing or sexual exploitation—could be bought at a luxury hotel designed in the Spanish or French style. Slave pens were rapidly hammered up and filled with people. Auctioneers, brokers and buyers gathered everywhere."[3] "Historically, the ballroom had served as a social center for extralegal system of placage, in which white men entered into domestic unions with women of African, Indigenous or mixed-race descent. . . . The white gentlemen would marry the women—they'd usually have white wives—but they'd put the women of color up in houses and provide for their care and that of their children. . . . It was an arrangement that was less violent than plantation rape but wholly predicated on white supremacy and patriarchy."[4] According to Perry, there are reminders of the trade in human flesh and the transport of unfree Black people all over New Orleans.

Louisiana also has the highest incarceration rate in the United States. The prison system is 66 percent Black, which is twice the rate of the Black population of the state. Perry wagers that perhaps the tendency for people in New Orleans to drink themselves to distraction is a consequence of the pain and grief that are ever present. According to Perry, New Orleans represents the

3. Imani Perry, "The Legacy of Slavery in New Orleans," *New York Times*, January 23, 2022, 10.
4. Perry, "The Legacy of Slavery," 10.

epicenter of the going and coming of people from Africa, the Caribbean, and Europe; New Orleans is a crossroad. Perry sums up the pain and pathos in a world where pain and grief are twins: "[In] Choctaw, the original name for New Orleans was Balbancha, meaning land of many tongues. . . . Africans, enslaved and free, from the continent, the upper South and the Caribbean have been coming for hundreds of years, now. New Orleans is a crossroads, and a cruel one. Waves of disaster and displacement—from chattel slavery to gentrification, from lynching to incarceration, and from one terrible storm to the next, have made it a fugitive place."[5]

## Loss of Self and Redemption Songs

I must confess that as a great-grandson of former enslaved persons from the Caribbean, I have visited Africa several times in attempts to trace my genealogical tree and have been surprised at how shallow are the roots of that tree. I recall sitting at breakfast with my host listening in awe to the symphonic tones of beautiful Ghanaian languages as they engaged in conversation. I was home in Africa, and yet I was excluded. The loss of language and culture made me feel rejected in my homeland. This loss of language and culture has been an immense obstacle to engage customs, rituals, and practices that would help in identifying streams of knowledge that would be useful in my search for roots. The painful truth is that I could not locate my roots, and I felt ashamed to have to settle with a strange name that does not honor my African ancestors. Perhaps this is an important aspect of what it means to be Black in the New World. It is having to live with the loss of one's language and culture, and a profound sense of helplessness when one's "back is against the wall" in the search for African identity. Invariably, we end up without a land or culture to call home. This is what it means to be black. Unlike our compatriots in suffering, First Americans, who when their backs are against the wall can find refuge and hope in their culture and re-

5. Perry, "The Legacy of Slavery," 10.

affirm a sense of identity, we have no such refuge. Orlando Patterson calls attention to the trauma of an African woman being stripped of her identity in the New World: "I was called up on one of her [Miss Ada's] birthdays, and Master Bob sorta looked out the corner of his eyes, first at me and then at Miss Ada, and then he made a little speech. He took my hand, put it in Miss Ada's hand, and say: 'Dis your birthday present, darling.' I made a curtsy and Miss Ada's eyes twinkle like a star, and she take me in her room and took on power over me."[6] One response to the loss of identity, the grinding poverty, and the inhumane conditions that confronted oppressed people in the New World was music—the power of the song served as a beacon of hope and an opportunity to change the cruel world of sin.

In an earlier chapter I called attention to Rastafari spirituality and the role of reggae music as a catalyst for changing the ethos and culture that shaped the lives of the poor throughout the Caribbean and now in much of the world. Reggae music became the means of a liberation ethic for Rastas and their lead singer, Bob Marley, in their commitment to "chant down Babylon." "Babylon" was a synonym for Western culture that oppressed the poor, especially the Black poor. It was through reggae and the power of the song that the oppressed poor inspired by Marley sought to transcend their local context and create an alternative reality. It is difficult to talk about Rastafari and reggae without reference to the consummate artist of this genre, Bob Marley. Through Marley's craft, reggae emerged as a Black cultural art form giving expressive power to voices long silenced by poverty, classism, and racial superiority, first in Jamaica, later throughout the Caribbean, and now in North America. Rastafari and reggae emerged in similar social settings. Both Rastafari and its music, reggae, emerged because Rastas belonged to the poor underclass in Jamaica who were excluded from polite society. Added to this was the sobering reality that for over three hundred years (1655–1962) Jamaica and many Caribbean nations existed as colonial outposts for Great Britain and other European nations. Don Taylor, a close associate of Marley,

6. Orlando Patterson, "The Constituent Elements of Slavery," in *Caribbean Slavery in the Atlantic World*, ed. Verene Shepherd and Hilary McD. Beckles (Kingston, Jamaica: Ian Randle Publishers, 2000), 38–39.

gives us a glimpse of the context in which he was raised and the social culture that informed his reggae music.

> Trench town and the rest of West Kingston were beginning to show a flare-up of the ghetto problem which had started to become noticeable in the early fifties: there were large tracts of waste land crammed with makeshift houses of itinerant rural squatters who captured every square inch of living space, as they moved from country to town. The shacks were built cheek-by-jowl and somehow the politicians thought the way to solve the problem was to bulldoze them all down and build large and concrete structures. . . . This was where Bob Marley ended up, in the area the country would later call concrete jungle.[7]

Reggae, like Rastafari, is woven into a "Black popular narrative." Through music the poor and marginalized find voice and are able to transcend their social context. Reggae, born in a context in which the first artists were seen as social outcasts, turned to a religious faith that was itself outside the mainstream, Rastafari. "Rastafarianism, whose roots are in Africa, in Jah, [God] Haile Selassie 1, the Emperor of Ethiopia. The themes of their message are rooted in the despair of dispossession, their hope is in Africa or diasporan solutions. As a result, their message emerges as ideology of social change."[8] Reggae music points to a clear option for the poor and powerless people who were excluded by church and culture because of their inability to climb the social ladder and be in a position to dress and have access to middle-class institutions. Through Reggae music piped into their homes via radio and, in more recent times, television, the forgotten poor began to learn that all people have inalienable rights and a responsibility to change their circumstance and affirm their dignity as sons and daughters of Jah (God). Those locked out of middle-class opportunities such as schools, churches, jobs, and housing for the poor were urged to "Get up and stand up for your rights." Marley

7. Don Taylor and Mike Henry, eds., *Marley and Me* (Kingston, Jamaica: Kingston Publishers, 1994), 23–24.
8. Carolyn Cooper, *Noises in the Blood* (London: Macmillan, 1993), 120–21.

captures this admonition in his song "No Woman No Cry." The theme of the song is that Jah is on the side of those who weep and are buffeted by poverty and crime. According to Marley, Jah takes sides with poor women who weep and are disabled by lack of jobs and homelessness. In Trench Town, where Marley lived, each day he would see hundreds of women who were unable to care for their children because they were landless and homeless. As far as Babylon (Western culture) is concerned, these women are invisible and without value. The reggae artist cries out (wails) on their behalf; Marley explains: "No one gives Jamaican people a chance, that's why we say the earth is corrupted and everyone has to die and leave we. . . . How long shall they pressure we? We are the people who realized the place where they thieved us from, so we say, ah, you took us from there, ah, this is where we are. . . . The greatest thing that could happen would never happen, so you could say God has we for a purpose."[9]

Through music the people begin to experience liberation as transcendence of life in Babylon as they begin to exit traditions that diminish their way of life. An ethic of liberation begins to emerge as Babylon begins to fall like the walls of Jericho. As sinister and final as Babylon appears to be, reggae music begins to craft an ethic of liberation grounded in biblical imagery. "Love to see when you move to the rhythm. . . . It reminds I of the days in Jericho. When we trotting down Jericho walls. These are the days when we'll trod through Babylon. Gonna trod until Babylon falls."[10] It was clear that for Marley and those edged out of "respectable society," liberation in Babylon was possible because Jah (God) lives. This was what made it possible for the poor and those who were excluded by the middle class to resist against the system in Babylon—they had confidence that, although they were sinned against, they would prevail because Jah lives. And so, Marley and a chorus of the poor and oppressed in Jamaica would wail—

9. Vivien Goldman, "Uptown Ghetto Living: Bob Marley in His Own Backyard," in *Reggae, Rasta, Revolution*, ed. Chris Potash (London: Schumer Books, 1997), 46.

10. Roger Steffens, "Bob Marley Rasta Warrior," in *Chanting Down Babylon*, ed. Nathaniel Samuel Murrell, William David Spencer, and Adrian Anthony McFarlane (Philadelphia: Temple University Press, 1998), 263.

Fools saying in their hearts,
"Rasta your God is dead"
But I and I know Jah, Jah!

. . . . . . . . . . . . . . . . . . . . .

Jah Jah live! Children yeah[11]


## Creation Story

Rastafari faith often makes appeal to Jah's creation of the world in an attempt
to call into question the present sinful and unjust conditions in the world.
Many Rastas, in their affirmation of the goodness of creation, recite Psalm
24, "The earth is the LORD's and the fullness thereof; the world, and they that
dwell therein . . ." (KJV). With this characteristic of Rastas to attribute value
to the divine creation, it should not surprise us that the consummate artist of
Rastafarianism, Bob Marley, in an attempt to lash out against the violence in
Jamaican and Caribbean societies, calls attention to the biblical doctrine of
creation. Biblical theologian Richard Middleton explains: "The other strategy is by appeal to creation, specifically to God's creational intent from the
beginning which can call into question the status quo, that is the present unjust order of things. Thus, we have Marley's famous song, 'One love.' . . . The
power of creation theology to sustain hope is evident in these lines found in
the very center of the song: As it was in the beginning (One love) so shall it
be in the end (One heart)."[12] "As it was in the beginning (One love) so shall
it be in the end (One heart)" revisits the purpose of creation. The purpose
is to lay aside violence against each other and the injustice that is rife in the
society. The purpose of creation is one love and one heart. It is the love of God

11. Bob Marley and the Wailers, "Jah Live," in *Songs of Freedom* (Tuff Gong, 1992); see
*The Complete Lyrics of Bob Marley: Songs of Freedom*, ed. Harry Hawke (London: Omnibus,
2001), 78.

12. Richard Middleton, "Identity and Subversion in Babylon," in *Religion, Culture, and
Tradition in the Caribbean*, ed. Hemchand Gossai and Nathaniel Samuel Murrell (New
York: St. Martin's, 2000), 191.

that constitutes the meaning and purpose of creation and calls the present order of injustice into question. It is God's love that brackets sin and gestures toward reconciliation with each other, with the uniting of hearts. The choice for all human beings is one love and one heart "because there is no hiding place from the father of creation." Marley's creation theology serves as a basis for hope in a culture and country where violence and injustice are the order of the day. And yet, according to the song, which is beyond the reach of the oppressor and of the violence in the society, there is hope for reconciliation and existence beyond sin and strife. Jah's purpose for creation is that creation would share one love and embrace one heart and certainly one song. The song is one of exodus, a call to leave oppressive traditions and histories as they embrace God's intent for creation. As Marley and the poor begin to chant down Babylon, "there is hope for the hopeless sinner."

### Love's Call Is Identical with Reconciliation

In January 1978, rival gunmen from the two main political factions in Jamaica arrived at Marley's temporary headquarters in England with a special request. A spontaneous truce had broken out in the ghettos of West Kingston, and to cement this momentous occurrence, a giant musical event called the "One Love Peace Concert" was to be held in Kingston on April 21, the twelfth anniversary of Haile Selassie's visit. The gunmen begged Marley to return to headline the event. He did, and on that evening, under a full moon in a jammed National Stadium, he implored "the two-leading people in this land to come on stage and shake hands, to show the people that you love them right, show the people that you gonna unite!" Leaping in a frenzy, Bob forced right-wing leader Edward Seaga to shake hands in public with the socialist prime minister, Michael Manley, a moment that has been immortalized in Jamaican mythology.[13]

Marley was instrumental in making the call to "One Love" the basis for a peace movement in Jamaica. He acknowledged the force of violence in gangs

13. Steffens, "Bob Marley Rasta Warrior," 260.

that sought to destroy each other. Inviting the two political leaders onstage to shake hands and announce to the people that they loved them acknowledged that human beings were meant and made for fellowship with each other and that sin engendered disruption and alienation not only with God, the source of life, but also with each other and with creation. In that concert, Marley helped the leaders of two political parties in Jamaica understand that they could say no to hate and violence that engendered separation from each other, from God, and from the land. Marley, in a classic "redemption song," reminds us that the song is beyond the reach of the oppressor and has the power and capacity to emancipate and liberate Jah's children as people of African descent unite. It was a powerful way to unite the Bible and Africa.

Marley, through his music and the power of the song, which was beyond the reach of the oppressor, acknowledged that a peace concert could not stem the tide of violence in Jamaica, throughout the Caribbean, and in the world, with a particular focus on North America. It was not lost on Marley that he was asked to host a peace concert in Jamaica while he was in London, England, to which he had fled because of the outbreak of violence in Jamaica. Marley was clear that the message of the peace concert, with its themes of love and peace, was the need to join the struggle in solidarity with the victims of violence and systemic oppression. The following year Marley released an album titled *Children Playing in the Street*. He complained about the plight of Jamaican children born in poverty and diminished by violence. Marley turned the spotlight on children and their suffering in Jamaican society. The liberation project was to be inclusive of women and children. This was of first importance in a patriarchal culture in which women and children were often seen but not heard from.

### Conversation with Dorothee Sölle

Marley's poetic renditions of his album *Redemption Songs* did not turn around the violence in Jamaica, the Caribbean, and much of the Third World, in which they are faithfully sung. What they did was provide a context for

53

reflection, and in fairness to Marley and the artists of reggae, this may also be said of the witness of the Christian church, which for two thousand years of reading the Bible and singing the songs of Zion may have to acknowledge that sin, "like a roaring lion, continues to devour God's children."

Dorothee Sölle, who has done an in-depth study of sin, expands Marley's view of sin against creation. One of the first observations that Sölle makes is that from a Christian perspective, sin should not be limited to a moral concept such as lying, stealing, murdering, or deceiving. Sölle acknowledges that while this is not to be condoned, sin is more than individual actions: "the fundamental sin, the primal sin—is something else: it is a state, not an action."[14] Another term for this fundamental or primal sin is "original sin." This is more than an individual breaching the divine law. It is the human opposition to life, or the sin against God's invitation to life. Sölle reminds us that in the final analysis, sin is also our decision; it is human beings saying no to God, and in a profound sense it is each of us exercising "free will." Sin, Sölle writes, is also "the destiny into which I was born. I am entangled in it through my parents, my teachers and my tradition. . . . While it is inappropriate to speak of collective guilt, the sense of collective responsibility for guilt is necessary. I am also responsible for the house which I did not build but in which I live."[15] According to Sölle and Marley, the place from which sin is recognized as sin must lie beyond sin. And this is one reason why sin and reconciliation are often paired. An analysis of the structures of sin already places us in a place beyond sin. This was the value and strength of Marley's *Redemption Songs*. And so, Marley wails from a place beyond sin as he proffers hope for liberation. Marley reiterates the plight that was the lot of Africa's children stolen from the homeland, yet with his reading of the Bible he concluded that sin was not the end of the story but that the hands of enslaved people and all who were oppressed by the powerful were strengthened by the hand of the Almighty, and that the divine presence gestured in the direction of reconciliation in spite of the precariousness that was the lot of the oppressed.

14. Sölle, *Thinking about God*, 54.
15. Sölle, *Thinking about God*, 55.

Marley combines sin and grace. Oppressed people who were denied their humanity by pirates survived because their hands were grasped by the hand of the Almighty. The enslaved survived and, in the end, thrived because they responded from a place beyond sin. Redemption songs were songs of grace. Sin talk must be conjoined with grace talk—talk of forgiveness and reconciliation. In a moment of revelation, Sölle proffers reflections on sin and grace. "It can be asked what function does talk of sin have, and for what is it used. It can be used in order to keep people down, keep them conscious of guilt and helpless, but it can also be thought of as an instrument for analyzing the situation, in which the aim remains the overcoming of the separation from the ground of life. Only if we stand with one foot already on the new land of forgiveness and grace do we talk rightly of sin."[16]

We must talk about sin from a place beyond sin. According to Sölle, this includes forgiveness and grace, and the acknowledgment that God's grace is more powerful than human wrong, and our theology should represent this. This does not obfuscate the claim and reality that we are all sinners. Yet, the divine action for us and in us provides us with redemptive space to critique sin. Sölle and Marley affirm the good news that we are more than captives to sin and its entrapments and forms of captivity in our world. We are more than consumers and purveyors of a culture enslaved to sin. We are created in the image of God. Although both Marley and Sölle affirm that this image of God in the human being has been defaced, deformed, and scarred, the good news is that we are sinners enabled by divine grace and offered, through love, the opportunity to begin again. Sölle reminds us that human beings live in the midst of a paradox—we are sinners and saints at the same time. Our search for God is simultaneously the search for self. Both Marley and Sölle remind us that human beings are creatures; we are limited. We have a beginning, and we have an end. We are in relationship with God, other human beings, the earth, and ourselves. We are created for fellowship with God, with Mother Nature, and with each other. It is at this point that Sölle reminds us that sin is an abrogation, a bracketing of this relationship. We experience sin as alien-

16. Sölle, *Thinking about God*, 58.

ation, with God, each other, and Mother Nature, which includes ourselves. Sin points to the disruption of the relationship, and at the same time, we long for a place beyond sin from which we can dream new worlds. Sin is the denial of our need for God, each other, and our world. To be created in the image of God is to acknowledge that, although we are hemmed in by sin and prone to its captivity, there is nonetheless an openness; the recognition of an invitation to embrace divine grace as an invitation to love God and be open to new life of friendship and responsibility with fellow human beings and Mother Earth. Our no to life is our embrace of sin and opposition to God's gift, grace.

## Grace Is Never Cheap

Black theologian J. Deotis Roberts reminds us of the inseparability of the cross of Christ and the Black religious experience. The cross of Christ for Black Christians is not only an attempt to look back two thousand years at the death of Christ that Christians imbue with salvific meaning. The cross of Christ became an existential experience that Christians lived each day. Roberts explains:

> The Black Christian knows that grace is never cheap. When I was a boy, I used to hear older blacks sing in the black church: "I wonder what makes this race so hard to run?" Those Christians knew the meaning of suffering. They knew that grace is never cheap. Blacks know what it means to suffer with Christ and to share his agony. . . . The rejection and shame of the crucifixion . . . is integral to the black experience. When I was a boy, I use to hear older people give gruesome details of lynchings that took place in our southern town in the presence of horrified blacks. They knew the meaning of cross bearing. As an adult, I too have known in my own experience what it means to endure harsh treatments and unmerited suffering in black skin in a racist society. In the midst of these experiences the cross has been to me a healing cross.[17]

17. J. Deotis Roberts, *Liberation and Reconciliation: A Black Theology* (Louisville: Westminster John Knox, 2005), 76.

Roberts reminds us that what makes the cross ours is that it is the cross of Christ. According to Roberts, the cross of the Black experience in the New World included lynching, rejection, shame, and crucifixion, and yet it became a healing cross because it was the cross of Christ. This was what turned the Christian understanding of the day Christ was crucified from a bad Friday into a good Friday. Although the suffering was extreme and intense, in the church in which I was baptized as a child we would sing on Sundays when the Lord's Supper was served,

> Nobody knows the trouble I've seen,
> Nobody knows but Jesus.
> Nobody knows the trouble I've seen,
> Glory, Hallelujah.

It was this identification with Christ as an expression of solidarity with Christ that made the cross of Christ a healing cross. No wonder the saints would sing, "There is power, wonder-working power in the cross of Christ." The pain of racism, sexism, homophobia, and systemic poverty was real, and the Black community witnessed to the anguish, misery, and death that were a result of struggling with the cross. And yet suffering and pain did not have the last word; as they embraced suffering as the suffering of Christ, the cross was transcendent and the community in solidarity with Christ asked: "Who is this Jesus who knows all about our troubles? Who is this Jesus who sees all our troubles?" The community, in solidarity with Christ, was clear:

> When I am dying, Be with me!
> When I am dying, Be with me
> When I'm on my lonesome journey
> I want Jesus to Be with me.[18]

18. Quoted in James H. Cone, *The Spirituals and the Blues* (New York: Seabury, 1972), 51.

This was the witness of the community in its discovery that Jesus the suffering servant was among us as community. The cross was alienating and engendered extreme pain as disciples separated from the community and as individuals sought to carry, so to speak, a private cross. As Christians acknowledge that they are called with others by Christ and begin to understand discipleship as fellowship with others, the cross becomes a healing cross. We no longer flee the cross of Christ, but, like Simon of Cyrene, we help Christ carry the cross in the midst of the world.

Roberts wrote his classic text *Liberation and Reconciliation: A Black Theology* (1971) three years after the death of Martin Luther King Jr. and two years after the publication of James Cone's first book, *Black Theology and Black Power* (1969). Because Roberts's book was a response to Cone's classic text, I will begin with a brief review of Cone's take on the doctrine of reconciliation and then pivot to Roberts's contribution.

## Liberation and Reconciliation

In his reflection "The Origin of Black Theology," James Cone points out that the impetus to write *Black Theology and Black Power* was to deal with the reality of being Black persons in a White racist society and to question why, although Christ made salvation possible for everyone, some are oppressed and segregated in churches and society on the basis of color. How can Whites claim Christian identity, which emphasizes the love and justice of God, and still support and tolerate the injustice committed against Blacks by churches and society? Why do Blacks accept White interpretations of society that deny their humanity and ignore their encounter of God (extending back to Africa) as liberator and protector of Black victims of oppression?[19]

Cone was ordained to the Christian ministry at age sixteen in the African Methodist Episcopal Church. He seems to have always had as a central ques-

19. James H. Cone, *For My People: Black Theology and the Black Church* (Maryknoll, NY: Orbis Books, 1984), 5–6.

tion the meaning of relating the gospel of Christ to the struggle of being a Black person in the United States. It became clear to him that God had turned to all human beings in the life, death, and resurrection of Jesus Christ and offered to all the gift of freedom. The task of the church was to proclaim the good news of freedom. As one of Cone's graduate students in the early 1970s, I recall vividly that he would always turn to Galatians 5:1: "For freedom Christ has set us free." The essence of the gospel according to Cone is the good news that Christ had set all people free, and yet the reality was that Black people were victimized and made captives in a racist society. The challenge was to find the power to break free from that captivity. It was Cone's notion of being held captive to segregation and the multiforms of racism that accentuated his passion to identify the means to set aside White supremacy—and the answer was Black power, the power to embrace freedom by "any means necessary," as he learned from Malcolm X, and to conjoin love with justice and power, as he learned from Paul Tillich. With Tillich, Cone asserted that "the new being" in Christ offered to Black people the option and necessity to affirm self as God's creation and child. Under the impact of the New Being, Black persons can affirm that "In a world which has taught blacks to hate themselves, the new Black man does not transcend blackness, but accepts it, loves it as a gift of the Creator."[20] Cone agreed with Tillich that love must be the foundation of power, and yet he was clear that the love he talked about included God's intentional purpose for humanity. Cone applied to the Black situation Tillich's insistence on the interrelationship of love, power, and justice as outlined in Tillich's book *Love, Power, and Justice*. "Taking his clue from Luther, Tillich speaks to the essence of Black Power and the uniqueness of Christianity when he says, 'It is the strange work of love to destroy what is against love.'"[21] An interpretive key for Cone was the interrelatedness of love, power, and justice that insists on a redistribution of power.

On the other hand, Cone uses the trinity of virtues—love, power, and justice—to embrace violence as a possible response of the Black community

20. James H. Cone, *Black Theology and Black Power* (New York: Seabury, 1969), 53.
21. Cone, *Black Theology and Black Power*, 54.

in an attempt to say yes to self, in an attempt to accept both self and neighbor. "If the riots are the black man's courage to say Yes to himself as a creature of God, and if in affirming self he affirms Yes to the neighbor, then violence may be the black man's expression, sometimes the only possible expression, of Christian love to the white oppressor."[22] Here Cone makes room for violence as a method of reconciliation, arguing that the means justifies the end. The end is both self and neighbor affirming Black existence, and this lays the basis for reconciliation between oppressed and oppressor. It is as the oppressed take steps that lead to liberation from self-denial that an opening for reconciliation with the oppressor is provided. It is liberation as interpretive key that provides a frame of reference for Cone with an openness for White people to become Black if they are to be reunited with the least of God's children, the Black community. The key here is that liberation and reconciliation include becoming Black. Cone, in his clearest statement concerning reconciliation, states:

> It is to be expected that many white people will ask: "How can I, a *white* man, become black? My skin is white and there is nothing I can do." Being black in America has very little to do with skin color. To be black means that your heart, your soul, your mind, and your body are where the dispossessed are. . . . Therefore, being reconciled to God does not mean that one's skin is physically black. It essentially depends on the color of your heart, soul, and mind. . . . The real questions are: Where is your identity? Where is your being? Does it lie with the oppressed blacks or with the white oppressors? Let us hope that there are enough to answer this question correctly so that America will not be compelled to acknowledge a common humanity only by seeing that blood is always one color.[23]

In the end, Cone seeks to avoid abstract ways of talking about oppressors and oppressed or Black and White persons. The only meaningful framework for

22. Cone, *Black Theology and Black Power*, 55.
23. Cone, *Black Theology and Black Power*, 151–52.

understanding the new humanity, or God's creational intent for humanity, is one's solidarity with the least of God's children. This is the pathway to reconciliation.

When Roberts happened on the world stage in 1971, in his book *Liberation and Reconciliation: A Black Theology*, he was received as a theologian of reconciliation, and this was new to Black theology. If the interpretive key for Cone was liberation, for Roberts it was reconciliation. It was clear that for Cone the breakthrough was relating the gospel of liberation to the social and political environment. In this context, the main key was liberation of the oppressed moving toward reconciliation. For Roberts, the point of departure was reconciliation in conversation with liberation. However, whether we listen to Cone or Roberts, the problems are the same—racism, sexism, persistent poverty, violence in the society, and death. Both Roberts and Cone affirmed the centrality of Black power, but they understood it differently. For Roberts it was the power that affirmed pride of place, dignity, Black pride, awareness, and self-determination. A distinction between Cone and Roberts is that Cone includes violence against all that would encroach on the well-being of Black persons. Cone says this: "The Christian does not decide between violence and non-violence, evil and good. He decides between less and the greater evil. He must ponder whether revolutionary violence is less or more deplorable than the violence perpetuated by the system. . . . Whether the American system is beyond redemption we will have to wait and see. . . . But we can be certain that Black patience has run out, and unless white America responds to the theory and activity of Black Power, then a bloody, protracted civil war is inevitable."[24]

Roberts agrees that, in part, his *Liberation and Reconciliation* is a response to key issues raised by Cone, and with Cone he affirms that the context in which they shared ideas in the 1960s and 1970s has changed. Roberts explains: "The balance between liberation and reconciliation remains essential in our pluralistic society. The multicultural emphasis now in vogue makes the urgency for genuine reconciliation more significant than

24. Cone, *Black Theology and Black Power*, 143.

before."[25] There is much agreement between Roberts and Cone. Both agree that the press for equality among the races and peoples fails to acknowledge the *imago Dei* as a point of departure for talk about human beings as daughters and sons of God. Cone frames the need for reconciliation among the races and among ethnicities as the call to solidarity, highlighting the preferential option of the poor and the call, so to speak, to become Black with the oppressed of the land. Roberts frames the need for solidarity and reconciliation in terms of equity, not equality. Roberts frames the issue as follows:

> Whites must now be ready to work with blacks for better racial understanding. Reconciliation must be based upon a one-ness in nature and grace between all people upon the principle of equity. Equality belongs to the time of integration. It assumes that blacks must earn the right to be equal—to be accepted into the American mainstream. Equity on the other hand belongs to the time of Black Power, black pride, awareness and self-determination. Equity assumes that all men are naturally equal. Human dignity is a birthright. Black theology affirms this and goes on to root equity as the only principle of black-white reconciliation, in the Christian understanding of creation and redemption.[26]

In his preface to the 1994 edition of *Liberation and Reconciliation*, Roberts mentions repentance as a necessary condition of reconciliation. However, in the main text of the 1971 edition, he does not call on White people to repent. Granted, he comes close to this in his insistent distinction between equality and equity. The emphasis on equality acknowledges that we all do not begin at the same place, and yet he does not yet highlight the systemic nature of the racism, sexism, and persistent poverty that is the lot of oppressed people. Cone seems to open the door not only for individuals to repent but for the state to repent for its sin of slavery against Black people. Cone frames

25. Roberts, *Liberation and Reconciliation*, xiii.
26. Roberts, *Liberation and Reconciliation*, 10.

the issue as follows: "White people have short memories. Otherwise, how are black people to interpret questions about reconciliation, love and other white values? Is it human to expect black people to pretend that their parents were not chattels in society? Do they really expect black people to believe that their status today is unrelated to the slavery of the past? Do they expect black people to believe that this society is not basically racist from top to bottom? . . . Black people can only speak of reconciliation when the black community is permitted to do its thing."[27]

In joining forces with Cone, Roberts questions whether Africa's children know themselves as their parents know them. Both remind us that Africa's children have a past, a past in which they have a culture in which there was a primacy of the community—"We are, therefore I am"—and an insistence that in the journey toward reconciliation the theological and the sociological must be conjoined. In *A Black Political Theology*, the follow-up text to *Liberation and Reconciliation*, Roberts gives sociological concreteness to systemic suffering in the Black community and reconciliation as the way to wholeness and the restoration of God's image among human beings and in creation writ large. According to Roberts, Africa's children were diminished and demeaned in the New World through White supremacy and the many ways in which the dominant culture in the New World oppressed Black people. People of African descent represent a past in which human beings are vitally related to nature, God, ancestors, and the community. Reconciliation must be multicultural, and the rupture with nature, God, ancestors, and the human family must be restored. Both Roberts and Cone seem to intimate that there is an aspirational and eschatological dimension to reconciliation, as Paul puts it in 1 Corinthians 13:12: "Now we see in a mirror, dimly, but then we will see face to face." The bottom line for Cone and Roberts is the need to begin to understand the transformed life in terms of God's intentional purpose for creation and affirm that in spite of the vagaries and malaise of sin expressed as racism, sexism, homophobia, and the multiforms of oppression in our world, God has not given up on God's creation. Transformation

27. Cone, *Black Theology and Black Power*, 144.

and the in-breaking of the new humanity are not dependent on the whims of the oppressor or the generosity of White people. For Cone and Roberts, liberation and reconciliation are the main keys in which Christian theology is set. Reconciliation is not proffered in a dialectical tension with liberation, but rather liberation becomes the motive force that provides the power for the community to claim God's creational intent for humanity.

One presupposition of the doctrine of reconciliation is the inclusive covenant that includes a multicultural society and leads the human family in the direction of the Beloved Community. The inclusive covenant that honors God's creational intent must insist that the means employed for the liberation of God's creation are consistent with the end desired. Because the end desired is a restored and reconciled society, the only appropriate means for struggle is nonviolence that will ensure that enemies will become friends and that instruments of hate cannot serve the goal of reconciliation. Reconciliation must mean more than integration; it means doing justice. Reconciliation must mean more than a change of heart. Change must be required in economics and politics. Change must be required in the foundations of society.

CHAPTER 3 ────────────────────────

# Baptism and the Mystery of Faith

In his classic text *The Blessing of the Holy Spirit*, J. E. Fison places a discussion of the Holy Trinity prior to his discussion of holy baptism. The discussion of the doctrine of the Trinity serves as a precursor, an introduction, to baptism, which is understood as an initiation into the mystery of God. The link between Trinity and baptism forces the initiate or the believer to take seriously the situation of faith, the world or the context in which one has to navigate the relationship between the triune God and one's entrance into the mystery of faith. According to Fison, at the heart of the doctrine of the Trinity is God's concern and demonstration of grace for humankind expressed in the divine participation in the world. In order to redeem the world back to God, God embraced the human condition. Fison puts it this way: "This, after all, is the very heart of the gospel of the incarnation. Only a Jew could reform Judaism creatively: only a Man [human being] could redeem mankind."[1] Fison is concerned that the participation of the divine in a world that had lost its way serves as a model for the one who is initiated into the life of the church to become redemptively and morally involved in the world. The situation, in which faith responds to the divine presence at work in the world, is one of estrangement. The human condition is estrangement from self, others, nature, and the divine; this is one reason many who participate in and are a part of the mystery called church feel so irrelevant and apathetic. "If we are to emerge from our pathetic irrelevance in the world today and rise above the mean and petty trifling which so often disfigures our witness to our Lord and His gospel, then we Christians need to realize afresh the benediction of the Triune Name, to the sound of which we constantly go forth from the church into the world."[2]

1. J. E. Fison, *The Blessing of the Holy Spirit* (London: Longmans, Green, 1950), 179.
2. Fison, *The Blessing of the Holy Spirit*, 181.

Because of the divine participation in the world, the church needs to acknowledge that, in spite of its problems, this is God's world; a world for which Christ died and one in which the Holy Spirit is at work calling God's children and creation away from sorrow and sin. According to Fison, to be human is to be called to take one's share and place in the world. Transformation happens in the world under the aegis of the divine presence. "Now the blessing of God the Father consists at least in this, that this world is His world, as much in its physical as in its moral and spiritual structure, nature and its laws as much as man [humanity] and his laws are ultimately in the hand of God."[3] One challenge is for humankind to accept its place in the divine order, being cognizant of the laws of nature and morality. There is a sense of lostness, a loss of one's rhythm with nature, of not being sure where we fit. One aspect of the tragedy that confronts the modern person is not being clear where he or she fits in the universe. There is a sense that it was this difficulty of not knowing how to make sense of the world, and one's participation in the church, that made the new initiate for baptism sing:

> Happy day, happy day,
> When Jesus washed my sins away!
> He taught me how to watch and pray,
> And live rejoicing every day;
> Happy day, happy day,
> When Jesus washed my sins away![4]

On the other hand, we took the biblical injunction seriously about "being in the world but not of the world," and so in preparation for baptism and at baptismal services we would sing, "The cross of Christ before us and the world behind us, no turning back, no turning back." In this song, to have the world on one's hands made one in the Black church sing about the need for prayer, the challenge to rejoice every day. There is a sense of

3. Fison, *The Blessing of the Holy Spirit*, 183.
4. Philip Doddridge, "O Happy Day That Fixed My Choice" (1755), found at Hymnary.org, accessed November 11, 2022, https://hymnary.org/text/o_happy_day_that_fixed_my_choice.

being alone drifting on the ocean of life, afraid and without a lifeboat. Fison asks for human beings to question their place in a law-abiding universe and acknowledge that this is the way to recover and, in some cases, discover "the peace of God which surpasses all understanding." However, there is a problem—challenges in the modern world that complicate the situation of faith. "The facts of science, the terrible and unpredictable hardships of nature, the universal suffering of mankind, and above all the hell of human sin that two world wars have revealed to us—in the face of these facts all talk of 'our heavenly Father' and a law-abiding universe is just wishful thinking."[5] Fison argues that if there is a problem from the human point of view in terms of the hardships of nature, human suffering, and the scourge of sin, there is on the other side a divine solution, which is summed up in the answer of salvation mediated through cross and resurrection. At the baptismal service, hope for a transformed life was signaled in the cross going before us. The way forward that Christianity presents is the actual lived experience of Jesus Christ expressed in his life, death, and resurrection. "It is here that the stubborn persistence of the crudest theories of penal substitution that have dogged consistently the attempts of the Christian church to explain the meaning of the atonement find their explanation, if not their justification. As theories, they are often immoral and quite untenable. Again, and again they transfer the essentially personal love of God in Christ 'reconciling the world unto himself' into the essentially impersonal wrath of God the Father appeased in some way of legal satisfaction by Christ."[6] Fison contends that the need for legal satisfaction in atonement theories, although crude, should not be set aside, because the atoning sacrifice of the divine wrath is in the New Testament. If on the one hand Golgotha seems to indicate that the world was turned upside down and law and order had taken an exit, the reality is that the resurrection of Christ witnessed to the Christian conviction that our hope was in Christ. This was still God's world. Through the life, death, and resurrection of Christ, God had provided an answer to suffering and sin.

5. Fison, *The Blessing of the Holy Spirit*, 183.
6. Fison, *The Blessing of the Holy Spirit*, 184.

Fison reminds us of the satisfaction theory developed by Anselm of Canterbury (1033–1109). In Anselm's theory God is presented as a king whose rights and honor have been violated by sin. Human beings are unable to offer satisfaction for their breach of relationship with God. Human beings violated the covenant with God, are culpable, and need to make amends to God but are unable because of their unworthiness. In response to this dilemma, God becomes human in Jesus and offers the life of Christ as a ransom. God in Jesus offers the required atonement for the breach in the covenant between the human community and God. Dorothee Sölle explains:

> This is a model of the need for the incarnation envisaged in juridical terms: Christ as the innocent victim submits to the will of the father and thus reconciles the father with us. Sometimes this notion is associated with the symbol of blood which washes us clean. Only blood can wash away transgressions. That the punishment we deserved is laid on the person of Christ then runs right through the whole of the Orthodox Christian tradition. We should really have been punished, but we were acquitted. Jesus Christ was punished, since he bore the suffering, the punishment, the damnation, indeed even the curse that we were under vicariously for us, and in this way redeemed us.[7]

Sölle points to connections between Martin Luther King Jr. and Fison, in King's assertion and belief in unmerited suffering. King believed that unmerited suffering voluntarily embraced had saving efficacy for society if society is to be redeemed from its manifold evils. The difference between King and Fison is that in King's position, it is not God who needs to be reconciled to human beings. Society needs to be reconciled; relationships among people need to be reconciled, bridging the gaps among peoples. However, both King and Fison agree that the way forward in terms of relationships and building bridges, whether on a cosmic or a human level, would be through Jesus and

---

7. Dorothee Sölle, *Thinking about God: An Introduction to Theology* (Harrisburg, PA: Trinity Press International, 1990), 122.

his cross. Both King and Fison agree that the hope for the transformation of the world is the recognition that God is the divine participant, who heard the groaning of God's children in Israel and sent Moses to demand that Pharaoh set free God's children. The hope for liberation, and healing, is ever present as the God of Christian faith is not the divine spectator but is at work in the world as creator, redeemer, and the spirit of freedom. "Above all, we must be reminded anew that God is at work in the universe. He is not outside the world looking on with a sort of cold indifference. Here on all the roads of life, he is striving in our striving. Like an ever-loving Father, he is working through history for the salvation of his children. As we struggle to defeat the forces of evil, the God of the universe struggles with us."[8]

Both King and Fison lead us in the direction of the making of a theology of solidarity. The identification of the divine with sinners occurs both in the incarnation of Christ and in the solidarity of Jesus with sinners both in his death and at baptism. The good news of the gospel is that the divine identifies with sinners in their struggle and hope for liberation and salvation. The divine humility is expressed in the incarnation as God in Jesus becomes human, and again at John's baptism for sinners as Jesus joins the crowd at the river Jordan. In solidarity with sinful humanity, Jesus demands that John the Baptizer, his cousin, immerse him. Baptism then becomes initiation into the mystery of the good news that God in the threefold nature of the Holy Trinity offers liberation and salvation. Anselm's theory of atonement pointed in the right direction, as he indicated that humanity was not able to pay the price for salvation, and God in Jesus paid the price for us. "Not with silver and gold, but with the life, death, and resurrection of Jesus Christ."

The central question for those growing up in the Caribbean was never freedom from ignorance but deliverance from the harsh suffering, grinding poverty, and sin, which was understood as the root cause of the suffering and poverty. "The bottom line is that people need to be free from sin. The church maintains that sin is the root cause of poverty, crime, social and economic injustice. Sin is not merely seen as a state into which everyone is born, but it is

---

8. Martin Luther King Jr., *Strength to Love* (Cleveland: Collins, 1963), 83.

understood as a destructive power that human beings cannot handle on their own. Seen as endemic and systemic, sin holds humanity in slavery. The wage sin pays is death, and the instrument of sin is the flesh, which points to our relationship with the world, our weakness and mortality."[9] The cardinal truth being explored is that it is futile and foolish to live *kata sarka* (according to the flesh), that is, relying on one's own strength and ingenuity. The history of New World slavery and the search for freedom teach that divine agency is crucial in the quest for liberation and salvation. "'You were bought with a price' (1 Cor. 6:20) is a popular text that speaks to this price as the purchase paid for the emancipation of the Jamaican people. God pays the ransom for our emancipation, a ransom we cannot pay for ourselves. Emancipation conjoined with revelation is seen as the breakthrough of grace."[10]

This imperative of emancipation and deliverance is also expressed in the Fourth Gospel, in the language of being born again. Jesus challenged Nicodemus, the ruler of the Jews, with the imperative for transformation: "You must be born again." The reply of the ruler of the Jews was on target: "Do you expect me to enter my mother's body and be born again?" The challenge that Jesus proffered highlighted the divine initiative, the priority of grace, as being born is not something we do for ourselves. The truth is that at birth we receive our lives as gift. Here was an accomplished ruler of the Jews who for so long had looked to the law and its observance as the way to salvation. Jesus turned this around for him by informing him that he had to receive new life as a gift of the spirit. You must be born of water and the spirit. Fison, in an intriguing argument about the priority of "water and spirit" as symbols of the transformed life, points out that in too many churches the centrality and priority of baptism is often forgotten; the individual replaces it with a decision in reference to Christ and soon forgets the priority of the work of the spirit of God in shaping the sanctified life. His argument is quite helpful, as he raises questions and issues concerning the place of the Holy Spirit in the renewal of life. Fison puts it this way:

9. Noel Leo Erskine, "How Do We Know What to Believe?" in *Essentials of Christian Theology*, ed. William C. Placher (Louisville: Westminster John Knox, 2003), 36.

10. Erskine, "How Do We Know?," 36–37.

"Ye must be born again"—this is our need too. It is not the eucharist and the corporate parish communion or the individual faith of a revived and deepened holiness that will provide the answer. It is only the "water and the spirit." After all, it is really futile to discuss Eucharistic controversies or the refinements of sanctification in the progress of the Christian life, if we have not come to grips with the terms of its commencement. It is therefore to holy baptism, the sacrament of the spirit, that we must look for the right answer as to how we too may regain contact with the living God. Only the spirit can make Christ our contemporary.[11]

Fison argues that the marginalization of baptism in the life of the church has led to the marginalization of the role of the Holy Spirit in the life of Christians. Baptism, he argues, is the sacrament of the Holy Spirit. On the one hand, he blames the marginalization of baptism for the emphasis of the liberal approach that reduces much of Christianity to an ethic of love, and thereby neglects the importance of baptism in the New Testament sense. On the other hand, baptism in the New Testament sense includes the entrance and presence of the Holy Spirit.

Then Jesus came from Galilee to John at the Jordan, to be baptized by him. John would have prevented him, saying, "I need to be baptized by you, and do you come to me?" But Jesus answered him, "Let it be so now; for it is proper for us in this way to fulfill all righteousness." Then he consented. And when Jesus had been baptized, just as he came up from the water, suddenly the heavens were opened to him and he saw the Spirit of God descending like a dove and alighting on him. And a voice from heaven said, "This is my Son, the Beloved, with whom I am well pleased." (Matt. 3:13–17)

Fison argues that although something new happened in the baptism of Jesus, it should be clear that he did not start a new tradition or a new movement. Jesus joined the revival of John the Baptist. "[Jesus] went down into

11. Fison, *The Blessing of the Holy Spirit*, 204.

the waters of John's baptism, down to the lowest place on the earth's surface and to the barren grimness of the lower Jordan valley, down to the eerie and symbolic and the very filthy and humdrum waters that flowed down in the middle of it."[12] We are reminded that the new birth involves baptism, and baptism includes water.

According to Fison, there is a distinction between Christian baptism in Spirit and John's baptism in water. "Water can at best only preserve the traditional. . . . It has no creative power. But the creative pattern can only spring out of the traditional and there can be no Christian baptism in Spirit without what is common to both Christian baptism, and John's baptism, and that common element is water. It is on the yonder side of water that we may contact Spirit and there is no other way."[13] Fison highlights an important insight: quite often Jesus did not discard Jewish tradition, but in submitting to it, he transformed it and something new emerged. The key to which Fison points, however, is that water is central to Christian baptism and is inadequate without the presence of the Spirit.

This comes to the fore in a conversation of the comparative merits of infant baptism and adult baptism. Fison points out that Baptists often place much emphasis on the ethical importance of change in behavior. In my Baptist tradition in Jamaica, as we prepared for baptism we would sing, "Things are different now, something happened to me, since I gave my heart to Jesus. Or again, things I use to do I do them no more." However, what is lost, according to Fison, is a sense of the mystical energy and presence of the Holy Spirit as the divine energy and mystical presence of God. What is often lost is a sense of the mystery of the salvation made possible by the work of the Holy Spirit, who makes Christ present. It is the mystery and miracle of the presence of the Spirit who makes baptism, whether infant or adult, a mystical encounter with the divine. Fison states the importance of the element of mystery in baptism clearly.

12. Fison, *The Blessing of the Holy Spirit*, 211.
13. Fison, *The Blessing of the Holy Spirit*, 212.

Indeed, there is a danger of isolated and pre-eminent emphasis on believers' baptism exclusively leading to the denial of the Spirit's essential self-effacement. There is something almost too clear, too simple, too understandable about the ideas of those who claim for adult baptism a clear-cut definition of meaning, which may not be claimed for infant baptism. Whatever we may think about the need for conscious decision for Christ by those who are of age to make such a decision—and the need is very great—yet it remains true that Christian initiation is as much a mystery for the adult as it is for the infant. Any attempt to eliminate the mystery from either baptism or confirmation will almost be treason against the Third Person of the Trinity.[14]

The point is well made of baptism as the sacrament of the Spirit, and there is an element of mystery as it pertains to the presence and power of the Spirit.

## Baptism as Witness to New Life

However, it is of first importance to note that baptism is not an end itself. It is witness to the presence of new life. Baptism is a symbol and manifestation of new life. Baptism is witness to the reality of new life made possible by the grace of God. Baptism is a witness to the reality of God's covenant with humanity, made clear in the church. God's promise and gift of new life are to the world, to humankind. Scripture informs us that God was in Christ reconciling the world unto God-self. The reality is that God's will was for humanity to be God's covenant partner throughout all eternity. This will of God is not clear to the world but made plain in the church, and, in his conversation with Nicodemus, Jesus indicates that the "new birth," which includes water and spirit, is necessary to see and enter the kingdom of God.

The eminent Baptist theologian G. R. Beasley-Murray, in his important book *Baptism Today and Tomorrow*, asks whether baptism should be under-

14. Fison, *The Blessing of the Holy Spirit*, 205.

stood as a sacrament or a symbol. He makes it clear at the very onset that as a Baptist he embraces the symbolic interpretation of baptism and does not understand baptism as a means of grace. Beasley-Murray cites Gerhard Kittel, a Lutheran theologian, and Karl Barth, a Reformed theologian, in his claim for the symbolic interpretation of baptism.

According to Kittel, "The chief mistake appears to me to lie in the fact that there is not a sharp enough distinction drawn between water baptism and Spirit baptism. It is never asserted in the New Testament that water baptism bestows the Holy Spirit, mortifies sinful lust or calls forth other spiritual changes. Everywhere it stands for an outward evidence that an inward transformation has been accomplished in a man."[15] Beasley-Murray points out that several denominations within the Christian church would agree with Kittel, since Calvinists subscribe to an understanding of sacrament as "an external sign, by which the Lord seals on our consciences his promises of good-will toward us, in order to sustain the weakness of our faith, and we in our turn testify our piety towards him."[16] According to Beasley-Murray, this definition of sacrament makes it difficult for anyone in the Calvinist tradition to understand Christian baptism as anything other than a symbol. Beasley-Murray points out that Karl Barth, in his definition of Christian baptism, speaks of baptism as symbolic: "Christian baptism is in essence the representation of a man's renewal through participation by the power of the Holy Spirit in the death and resurrection of Jesus Christ, and therefore with the representation of man's association with Christ, with the covenant of grace which is concluded and realized in Him, and with the fellowship of his Church."[17]

Beasley-Murray highlights Barth's use of the word "representation." This means that for Barth baptism is a representation, a picture, a witness, a sign

---

15. G. Kittel, "Die Wirkungen der christlichen Wassertaufe nach dem Neuen Testament," *Theologische Studien und Kritiken* 87 (1914): 25, cited in G. R. Beasley-Murray, *Baptism Today and Tomorrow* (New York: St. Martin's, 1966), 16.

16. Beasley-Murray, *Baptism Today and Tomorrow*, 17.

17. Beasley-Murray, *Baptism Today and Tomorrow*, 17, citing Karl Barth, *The Teaching of the Church regarding Baptism* (London: SCM, 1948), 9.

of salvation made possible by Jesus Christ and the participation of believers in this rite. Beasley-Murray cites Barth's continuation of the earlier passage: "So far as I know there is no teaching about Christian baptism which would directly contest the view that water baptism itself is also, and indeed primarily, to be understood as a symbol, that is, as a type, and a representation or, according to Gregory of Nyssa, a copy of that other divine-human reality which it attests."[18]

Barth rejects notions of baptism as a means for imparting forgiveness of sins and the Holy Spirit. This is in direct contrast to the earlier position advocated in this chapter by the Anglican theologian J. E. Fison. According to Fison, there is an indissoluble link with water and Spirit. "The word, water, links the new birth indissolubly with baptism and the word, spirit, links it indissolubly with the new element introduced into the meaning of the rite at Jesus' own baptism. It is the descent of the Spirit at his baptism that really justifies the Matthaean baptismal formula, 'baptizing . . . into the name of the Father and of the Son and of the Holy Ghost.'"[19]

A central theme that Beasley-Murray underscores is that baptism is not the means of grace that imparts forgiveness or the source or cause of our salvation. Baptism is a sign, a witness of the new knowledge of salvation.

Anders Nygren, in his *Commentary on Romans*, points out that Paul places the conversation in the context of the relationship between Christ and Adam. The person who has been baptized into Christ has been accepted and received into a real fellowship of death and life in him.

> "In Adam" we all belonged to the same organism. As human beings we are members of *one* body, which, through its head, Adam, stands under the reign of sin and death. That which is true of the head is also true of each member of the body. All participate in Adam's sin and in Adam's death. But now, through baptism, we have been incorporated into Christ. That means that we are henceforth not merely members in the great organism

18. Beasley-Murray, *Baptism Today and Tomorrow*, 17.
19. Fison, *The Blessing of the Holy Spirit*, 206.

of humanity; we are members in "the body of Christ." "By *one* Spirit we were all baptized into *one* body" (1 Cor. 12:13).[20]

According to Nygren, what was true concerning humanity in its relationship to Adam is *even more true of humanity in relationship to Christ, when humanity becomes a part of the body* of Christ. "Christ's death is our death, and Christ's resurrection is our resurrection. It is of this fellowship of death and life with Christ, established through baptism, that Paul speaks of when he says, 'Do you not know that all of us who have been baptized into Jesus Christ were baptized into his death? We were buried therefore with him by baptism into death, so that as Christ was raised from the dead by the glory of the Father, we too might walk in newness of life' (Romans 6:3–4)."[21] We are reminded that baptism includes the risk of death, as the person who is immersed in water signifies the experience of death with Christ. The person who comes up out of the water signifies the experience of new life "with Christ."

Nygren argues that the signifying of the believer with Christ in burial and the gift of new life should not be understood as "symbolical" in terms of how this word is used. He puts it this way: "But it would be an utter misinterpretation if, for that reason, one were to characterize Paul's view of baptism as 'symbolical,' in the sense in which the word is generally used. For, according to Paul, in baptism we have to do with realities, not merely with symbolical representations. That which baptism symbolizes also actually *happens*, and precisely through baptism."[22] According to Nygren, Paul emphasizes facts such as we who were baptized are united with Christ, "in a death like his and . . . a resurrection like his" (Rom. 6:5). The point here is, believers became united to Christ through baptism and belong in the new humanity of which Christ is head. "Through baptism we have been received into the new age, which began in the resurrection of Christ. He who has been baptized into Christ has been incorporated into Him; he is

20. Anders Nygren, *Commentary on Romans* (London: SCM, 1958), 232–33.
21. Nygren, *Commentary on Romans*, 233.
22. Nygren, *Commentary on Romans*, 233.

'in Christ.' . . . He who, through baptism, is in Christ is a new creation, a new man, formed according to the nature of the new aeon."[23] Nygren is insistent that we do not need symbolic language to characterize the relationship of the believer to Christ. He proffers a language of reality that is based on a relationship that the baptized has with a real person, Jesus of Nazareth, "who lived on earth, suffered under Pontius Pilate, was crucified, dead and buried, and on the third day rose again from the dead. It is with Him that we, through baptism, have been incorporated; and what we share with Him is just that which befell Him during his life on earth, in time and space."[24]

Both Beasley-Murray and Barth proffer the understanding that baptism in the New Testament points to a symbolic representation of the relationship between the believer and Christ. Baptism signifies death and new life, burial and resurrection, and there is no intrinsic connection between water and spirit as is claimed by the Anglican theologian J. E. Fison. Water as such points beyond itself as it symbolizes a new relationship between the believer and Christ that is witnessed to by the baptismal experience. One of the strengths of the symbolic interpretation of baptism is that it makes room for the baptism of infants, who are unable to verbalize or consciously witness to the experience of death and new life that the sacramentalists claim *happens* in time and space. Fison indicates that one of the gifts that the sacramentalists offer in the baptismal rite is the sense of mystery made palpable in uniting the initiate with Christ. And the sense of mystery is real as the presence of the Spirit of Christ is contemplated, whether infants or believers are being baptized.

On the other hand, Nygren highlights both a negative and a positive side to baptism. This conjures up images of the divine and human side of a discussion of the church or of the doctrine of Christ. Of course, the language of negative and positive does not apply to the two natures of Christ, unless one is an "adoptionist" who sees the human side of Christ

23. Nygren, *Commentary on Romans*, 235.
24. Nygren, *Commentary on Romans*, 238–39.

as inferior to the divine side. On the other hand, one could wager that the sins that are attributed to the church, because it is a human institution, are a result of the human side and not the divine. But this excursus aside, Nygren states that there is a negative side to the believer that needs to be crucified and a positive side that needs to experience resurrection. The point that Nygren wants to underscore as a sacramentalist is that this is not symbolic language, but that sin (*kata sarka*) must be crucified and the believer must be united with Christ in a *resurrection* like his. He puts it this way:

> This crucifying of the old man, this destroying of the sinful body, is, however, only the negative side of baptism. It is that of which Paul says, "We have been united with him in a *death* like his." But baptism also has its positive side; we are also "united with him in a *resurrection* like his." Through baptism the place of "the old man" has been taken by "the new man," by the man who belongs to "the new aeon" and is characterized by its nature. . . . He who, through baptism, is in Christ is a new creation, a new man, formed according to the nature of the new aeon. . . . The central thought for Paul, when he speaks of baptism, is thus *the participation of the baptized in the death and resurrection of Christ.*[25]

In his pivotal text *Paul and His Letters*, New Testament scholar Leander E. Keck theorizes that Saint Paul did not make baptism central to his mission of proclaiming the gospel of Christ, as he assumed that his readers were all baptized. However, Keck is careful to assert that baptism was nonetheless an important key in his proclamation of the gospel of Christ, as baptism was an important response that Paul sought. Further, Keck points out that Paul was unaware of the tradition in Matthew 28:16–19 in which the risen Jesus commissioned his apostles to baptize, in the name of the triune God. Keck enumerates practices of baptism among the early Christian community in Paul's time.

25. Nygren, *Commentary on Romans*, 235–36.

1. According to Keck, Christians did not invent baptism, nor did the practice begin with Jesus. Christians baptized those who accepted their message. There are good reasons to infer that the Christian practice goes back to John the Baptist.

2. Baptism was an initiation into the Christian community. This may account for the reason why in many churches the baptistery is at the entrance of the church.

3. Baptism in the early church and in the time of Saint Paul was apparently by immersion. The rite itself was accompanied by confession and administered "in the name of Jesus" (Acts 2:38; 1 Cor. 1:13); baptism in the name of the Father and the Son and the Holy Spirit was added later (Matt. 28:19).

4. The problem of whether to baptize infants of Christian parents was not an issue in Paul's time. Persons who were baptized along with their households confessed Jesus as Lord (Acts 16:15).

5. Keck's pivotal claim is that it is most unlikely that any Christian in the early church would have regarded baptism "merely as symbol," that is, as an action whose efficacy lay outside of the act of baptism. "Rather, for the ancients in general, rites actually did something; the action had power. In other words, it is likely that early Christians regarded baptism as a sacramental act."

6. Christians in the early church believed that the gift of the Holy Spirit was concurrent with baptism. In the early church, this gift was received by every baptized believer.[26]

Fison argues that what was new in Christian baptism was the receiving of the gift of the Holy Spirit. Indeed, what differentiated Christian baptism from the baptism of John the Baptist was the presence of the Holy Spirit, who appeared at the baptism of Jesus. There is, so to speak, a new point of departure with Christian baptism, and this is evidenced by the creative presence of the Holy Spirit. It should not surprise us, then, that Fison led into a discussion of holy baptism with a discussion of the threefold gift of the Holy Trinity, and it is the benediction of the "Father Almighty" with gifts of

26. Leander E. Keck, *Paul and His Letters* (Philadelphia: Fortress, 1988), 55.

creation, redemption, and reconciliation that equips the church at worship to enter the world with a readiness to serve in the name of the triune God.

## Toward Paul's Theology of the Cross

On the other hand, Keck, who, like Fison, proffers a sacramentalist view of baptism among early Christians in the time of Saint Paul, wagers that Paul was not aware of the baptismal formula mentioned in Matthew 28:19. According to Keck, baptism in the early church was in the name of Jesus. If what was new in the act of Christian baptism for Fison was the gift of the Spirit and the two central prerequisites for Christian baptism were water and the Holy Spirit, Paul would have understood baptism quite differently, according to Keck. The new that Paul introduced to Christian baptism was the participation of the believer in the death of Jesus Christ. Keck suggests that Paul may not have invented this focus on the believer at baptism participating in the death of Christ. Paul suggests as much in Romans 6:3: "Do you not know that all of us who have been baptized into Christ Jesus were baptized into his death?" This view was already held in the church at Rome.

Keck illustrates how as modern people we may understand what it means to participate in the death of Christ in spite of the challenge of our penchant to think as individuals.

> Such an understanding of baptism is possible only if "Christ" is understood in a particular way. In Rom. 5:12–21, Paul had contrasted Adam and Christ, not simply as individuals but also as "corporate persons"—persons who, without losing their individuality, included others. It is exceedingly difficult to conceptualize this because our thinking is profoundly individualistic. . . . Something of an analogy may be useful, however. Blacks often sensed that what happened to Martin Luther King, Jr., was happening to them as well. When he was at the White House, they were there; when he was shot, they were shot. This analogy may be suggestive, but it also has clear limits, for Dr. King was a symbolic representative of the whole. For

Paul, however, Christ and Adam were more than representative figures, ones who "stood for" a group. They embodied the group and determined its fundamental character.[27]

The key here is that whoever is baptized into Christ has "put on" Christ. "There is no longer Jew or Greek, there is no longer slave or free, there is no longer male and female; for all of you are one in Christ Jesus. And if you belong to Christ, then you are Abraham's offspring" (Gal. 3:28–29).

Keck points out that highlighting the believer participating with Christ in baptism, Paul emphasizes the center of his Christology as "cross and resurrection." "Paul never says that the baptized participate in Christ's post-existent glory, let alone his divinity. Rather, in keeping with his focus on the cross, he says that those who were baptized were 'baptized into his death' [Rom. 6:3]."[28] According to Keck, what is at stake here is a sacramental move by Paul insisting that the believer is united with Christ in baptism. However, although Paul speaks of the baptized person participating in Christ's death, he does not speak of unification of the believer and Christ in terms of resurrection. Paul does not speak of the believer participating in Christ's resurrection through baptism. "In Rom. 6:8 we read, 'But if we have died with Christ [as indeed we have] we believe that we shall also live with him.' Participation in Christ's resurrection is future. One reason the letters to the Colossians and Ephesians are considered to be deutero-Pauline is that they regard participation in Christ's resurrection as something already experienced (Col. 3:1; Eph. 1:20). In Rom. 6:4, on the other hand, we read, 'We were buried . . . with him . . . so that as Christ was raised from the dead . . . we too might walk in newness of life.'"[29] A point Keck seeks to underscore here is that the resurrection of Christ is the basis of a new moral life.

James Cone goes further than Keck, in giving sociological depth and concreteness to the conjoining of the believer and Christ in the reality of baptism and resurrection. Cone reminds us that baptism was a historical event that

27. Keck, *Paul and His Letters*, 56.
28. Keck, *Paul and His Letters*, 57.
29. Keck, *Paul and His Letters*, 57.

happened in real time in which Jesus submitted himself to John's baptism so that he may enter into solidarity with oppressed people. Although Cone does not use the term "sacrament of solidarity," it is clear that this sentiment is not far from his emphasis on the immersion of Jesus in the community of the poor and neglected. Jesus's solidarity with the poor announces that the kingdom of God is for the poor and oppressed and not for the rich and haughty. "In baptism Jesus embraces the condition of sinners, affirming their existence as his own. He is one of them! After the baptism, the saying, 'Thou art my beloved Son; with thee I am well pleased' (Mark 1:11) expresses God's approval of that very definition of Jesus' person and work."[30]

In his depiction and portrayal of the baptism narrative, Cone focuses not on the act of believers being baptized and their relationship with Christ but on the meaning of Christ's participation with the multitudes at John's baptism. Cone's focus is on the identification of Jesus with the oppressed and its symbolism in terms of liberation.

If according to Keck cross and resurrection were interpretive keys for Saint Paul as he sought to explicate the unification of the believer in the death of Christ through baptism, Cone uses these keys of cross and resurrection to show the unity of Christ with the community of the oppressed in their struggle for liberation and freedom. Cone puts it this way:

> The theological significance of the cross and resurrection is what makes the life of Jesus more than just the life of a good man who happened to like the poor. *The finality of Jesus lies in the totality of his existence in complete freedom as the Oppressed one who reveals through his death and resurrection that God is present in all dimensions of human liberation.* His death is the revelation of the freedom of God, taking upon himself the totality of human oppression; his resurrection is the disclosure that God is not defeated by oppression but transforms it into the possibility of freedom.[31]

30. James H. Cone, *A Black Theology of Liberation* (Maryknoll, NY: Orbis Books, 2005), 115.
31. Cone, *A Black Theology of Liberation,* 118.

There is a difference here between Cone and Paul as it pertains to oppressed communities in their search for freedom. According to Keck, salvation or new creation is made possible through the embodiment of the believer in Christ. The believer participates in the death of Christ and shares in the new life made possible by Christ. Keck insists that, for Paul, the believer does not share the resurrection event with Christ—that will be an eschatological happening for the believer.

It is significant that in this context Cone does not lay stress on the oppressed person joining with Christ; rather, Christ, through death and resurrection, defeats death and opens the door to fuller and more meaningful life. Cone seems to suggest that Christ is the representative who acts on behalf of the oppressed and makes possible their entry into newness of life. But according to Keck, Paul's emphasis is more organic and embodied. Christ is not just the representative person but the corporate person, as was also true of Adam. Human beings participated in Adam's fall, and the human family shared in that misstep and suffered a fall. However, the converse is equally true: because humankind is also a part of the corporate reality of Christ, we do not only share in his death through baptism but will also share in the new life resurrection makes possible. Here indeed is a stark contrast between the language of representation and the language of embodiment. Paul captures it succinctly in 2 Corinthians 5:17: "So if anyone is in Christ, there is a new creation: everything old has passed away; see, everything has become new!" And again, in Galatians 3:27–29: "As many of you as were baptized into Christ have clothed yourselves with Christ. There is no longer Jew or Greek, there is no longer slave or free, there is no longer male and female; for all of you are one in Christ Jesus. And if you belong to Christ, then you are Abraham's offspring."

Even though Cone shares with Barth a focus on Christ as the representative who took on the forces of death and sin and made it possible for liberation and salvation to become a reality, there seems to be a more nuanced focus in Barth of highlighting Christ as representative and the Holy Spirit as the energy and power of Christ who enables the participation of the believer in Christ. Cone states the issue clearly for us: "For men and women who live in an oppressive society this means that they do not have to behave as if *death* is the ultimate. God in Christ has set us free from death, and we can now live without worrying about social ostracism, economic insecurity, or political tyranny. 'In Christ the immortal God has tasted death and in so doing . . . destroyed death' (Hebrews 2:14ff.)."[32] The good news here is that God has acted on our behalf in Christ Jesus. This means that divine agency is operative on our behalf. Death no longer has the last word because its power is broken. Oppressed persons now have the courage to face the enemy and are able to say no to oppression because, according to Cone, God has said yes to them. How then may we understand resurrection? "To believe in the resurrection transforms faith from a deliverance from the world into an initiative that transforms the world and makes those who believe into worldly, personal, social and political witnesses to God's righteousness and freedom in the midst of a repressive society and an unredeemed world. In this, faith comes to historical self-consciousness and to the recognition of its eschatological task within history."[33]

Professor Cone complexifies the relationship between the individual and Christ, as Cone does not want to limit the relationship of the oppressed community to the baptized community. Soteriology, traditionally understood as church membership, is not an adequate category for interpreting the relationship of the oppressed to Christ. While Cone presses beyond soteriology as traditionally understood, he goes beyond the institutional church and does not limit salvation to church membership. However, he does not yet anchor salvation in the context of the doctrine of creation. Cone is conflicted as to whether Jesus the Christ sets the standard for what it means to be Black. On the one hand, Cone states that Jesus is the oppressed one par excellence, who sets the standard of what it means to become Black, yet on the other hand, if Christ is not as Black as the Black community, out of concerns for being Black, Black people or the oppressed community must abolish Christ. Cone puts it this way: "The black community is an oppressed community

32. Cone, *A Black Theology of Liberation*, 118.
33. Cone, *A Black Theology of Liberation*, 119.

primarily because of its blackness; hence the Christological importance of Jesus must be found in his blackness. If he is not black as we are, then the resurrection has little significance for our times. Indeed, if he cannot be what we are, we cannot be who he is. Our being with him is dependent on his being with us in the oppressed black community, revealing to us what is necessary for our liberation. The definition of Jesus as black is crucial for Christology if we truly believe in his continued presence today."[34]

On the one hand, in the baptismal metaphor Paul makes the case of the believer participating in the death of Christ and rising in newness of life. It is clear that for Paul Christ is normative in talk about cross and resurrection, and the baptized person through participation enters the domain of Christ and thereby shares and participates in newness of life. Cone is able to argue that the situation of faith dictates the way forward, and that situation is one of racism, sexism, classism, and militarism in which the humanity of God's children is compromised and set aside. The existential situation is an emergency situation, in which the point of departure for what God is up to in the world is found in the oppressed condition to which Christ is not a stranger, as the story of his birth, life, and death is indeed a testimony. Cone knows this intuitively and captures this sometimes in the declaration of Jesus in Matthew 25:40: "As you did it to one of the least of these who are members of my family, you did it to me." Here the relationship between Christ and the oppressed is without contest. There is no daylight between them. Cone turns this around and suggests that the Resurrected One will become existentially irrelevant if he is not related to the oppressed Black community. The problem here is that Cone is working with a binary approach to the reality of Jesus the Christ and his relationship to humanity. What if Christ and the community cannot be separated? What if there is an interrelationship between Christ and the oppressed community? If some understanding of cross and resurrection is at the very heart of the community of the crucified, then Cone does not have to doubt that the Christ at its center may be an impostor. Paul captures this in Galatians 2:19–20: "I have been crucified with

---

34. Cone, *A Black Theology of Liberation*, 120.

Christ; and it is no longer I who live, but it is Christ who lives in me. And the life I now live in the flesh I live by faith in the Son of God, who loved me and gave himself for me."

Cone illustrates his dilemma of holding together the divine initiative, on the one hand, and human agency, on the other hand. "The blackness of Christ clarifies the definition of him as the *Incarnate One*. In him God becomes oppressed humanity and thus reveals that the achievement of full humanity is consistent with divine being. The human being was not created to be a slave, and the appearance of God in Christ gives us the possibility of freedom."[35] The major problem in Cone's methodology is that he suggests that Christ should become Black with the oppressed. The problem clarified by his mentor Karl Barth is that Cone, unlike Saint Paul and Barth, separates cross and resurrection. It is clear that for Cone baptism is a symbol of the relationship between the oppressed and Christ, but Cone is not confident that the oppressed should become Black with Christ. Cone is unclear if it is Christ who identifies with the oppressed or if it is the oppressed who identify with Christ. There are times when he suggests that Christ must become Black like the oppressed, or he will be abolished. This is one of the risks with Cone's methodology; it makes the Black experience normative for theology. The risk that Cone joins is that of deifying the Black experience and raising the possibility that if the Black experience does not recognize Christ, he has to be abolished. Perhaps a more appropriate starting point is an understanding of prevenient grace. What if in the image of the Good Samaritan Christ has taken on the condition of the oppressed and invites us to join him? What if we are called to become Black with Christ?

Cone, in his *God of the Oppressed*, suggests that there is much the Black church could learn from Karl Barth, and while Barth would have problems with the notion of a Black Christ, his use of the doctrines of cross and resurrection and the priority of the history of the church as source may be instructive:

35. Cone, *A Black Theology of Liberation*, 121.

What baptism portrays, according to the basic passage in Romans vi. 1f., is a supremely critical happening,—a real event whose light and shade fall upon the candidate in the course of his baptism. This happening is his participation in the death and resurrection of Jesus Christ: that is, the fact that at a particular time and place, in the year A.D. 30 outside Jerusalem on the cross at Golgotha, not Jesus Christ alone, but with Him also this particular individual died eternally, and that, in the garden of Joseph of Arimathea, not Jesus Christ alone, but with Him also this particular individual died eternally, and that, in the garden of Joseph of Arimathea, not Jesus Christ alone, but with him also this particular individual rose from the dead for evermore.[36]

There are profound differences between Cone's and Barth's approach to Christology and soteriology. Cone's point of departure is the Black experience and a conversation about God and humanity that is accountable to this community. Barth's conversation is from the context of the Christian church and in conversation with church history and notions of revelation. Barth could learn many things from Cone's approach, for example, the centrality of the Jewishness of Jesus and its importance for the concreteness of theological discourse, and the importance of giving care to the particularity of the situation of faith. From the perspective of Cone, Barth's conjoining of cross and resurrection, the location of the cross-resurrection discourse within history, and more of a focus on the universality of the liberation and salvation that God offers in Jesus Christ are notes that could be instructive.

This would save Cone's theological discourse from valorizing the Black experience and thereby running the risk of idolatry. What if at the end of the day salvation and liberation find their energy in the oppressed who are situated in the domain of Christ through participation in Christ's death and resurrection to newness of life? What if baptism in the death and burial of Christ and the gift of new life made possible by Christ's resurrection are the source, and not the Black experience?

36. Barth, *The Teaching of the Church*, 11 (emphasis removed).

Frederick Herzog, in his important book *Liberation Theology: Liberation in the Light of the Fourth Gospel*, joins the discussion about the relevance of the Black experience as a mode of liberation. Herzog turns the spotlight on Nicodemus's meeting with Jesus and announces that the invitation of Jesus to be born again was an invitation to become Black. According to Herzog, Nicodemus did not understand the mission of Jesus and approached Jesus as a God-sent teacher with whom God dwells. Undoubtedly he was impressed with the ministry of Jesus and had a sense that God was with Jesus, otherwise Jesus would not be such a great teacher. Herzog paraphrases the response of Jesus to Nicodemus.

> In response, Jesus revamps Nicodemus' world-view. He offers a new idea. What it involves in our day is plain: "Believe me, no man can see the kingdom of God unless he become black" (v.3). Doesn't the idea sound absurd? How can a man become black when he is white? Can he again enter his mother's body and be born different? (v.4). Jesus' reasoning is based on another logic: "Believe me, if a person is not born of water and Spirit, he cannot enter the kingdom of God. Flesh creates flesh, and spirit creates spirit" (vv.5–6). Nicodemus is still arguing on the ground of wanting to retain white superiority, private selfhood. Jesus is concerned about a different self, corporate selfhood, which man controls as little as the wind (v.8). Here the brutal logic of retaining one's identity as the superior white self or the "private I" no longer prevails.[37]

Herzog introduces an element of mystery: "to be born again, or to be born anew," was a work of the Spirit and was related to the kingdom of God. In a profound sense, a part of the new reality that Jesus introduces, and that baffled Nicodemus, had to do with the in-breaking of the kingdom of God. Indeed, a sign and signal of the in-breaking of the kingdom was the gift and the aegis of the Holy Spirit. Herzog joins the conversa-

37. Frederick Herzog, *Liberation Theology: Liberation in the Light of the Fourth Gospel* (New York: Seabury, 1972), 62–63.

tion at this point as he infers that Nicodemus could not understand the meaning of "being born again" as an outsider. Being born again is the work of the Spirit, and the Spirit cannot be controlled; the Spirit is like the wind. Jesus understood being born again as the work of the Spirit. Understanding the phenomenon of the work of the Spirit has to happen from the vantage point of the kingdom of God. And according to the Gospel of Saint Mark, Jesus walks into town and announces that the kingdom of God is in the midst of the people. "Now after John was arrested, Jesus came to Galilee, proclaiming the good news of God, and saying, 'The time is fulfilled, and the kingdom of God has come near; repent, and believe in the good news'" (Mark 1:14–15). The problem with Nicodemus was that the context from which he sought to understand this new happening announced by Jesus as new life, new birth, was Jewish tradition and Jewish law. The invitation to Nicodemus by Jesus was to enter the new sphere, the new vantage point of the kingdom of God, which was not limited to Israel but now in Christ was available through participation in the death and resurrection of Christ.

Herzog, in the tradition of Cone, seeks to contextualize the new reality announced by Jesus to the Jewish leader. According to Herzog, the new that Jesus represents and to which Jesus invites Nicodemus is as radical as a White man enmeshed and besmirched by racism attempting to be in solidarity with the Black community. One problem is the understanding of the self as private and the location of the White self in the context of White power, or some notion of the self in the context of religion and capital. What Jesus did in driving the money changers out of the temple in an attempt to cleanse his Father's house is also true of a faithful understanding of the self. The self needs to be cleansed, because what is at stake is an understanding of the self as the temple of God, the temple in which we worship God. Herzog puts it this way: "The Fourth Gospel presupposes that man has been enslaved in a false relationship toward himself, a false self, a private self. Jesus' open way of acting confronts man with a corporate selfhood. It challenges men to begin anew with being human. But beginning over again is not a matter of course.

It calls for radical change, liberation of consciousness. Man is asked to grasp his selfhood anew."[38]

The challenge of human beings in relation to the call and challenge of Christ to become Black is, one has to be born again. The invitation to the kingdom of God is an invitation to transformation and liberation of the private self to participate in the corporate selfhood of Christ. To enter the kingdom of God is to become Black with Christ. In the language of Paul Lehmann, in his classic text *Ethics in a Christian Context*, the challenge that confronts humanity in the search to become human is to join Christ in the mission and task of "making human life human and keeping human life human." Is this what it means to become Black with Christ? The call to become Black is offered to all who will give up private selfhood, step aside from seeing life from worldviews that sacralize the relationship between capital and religion, or domination of men over women, or the desecration of human beings who choose to love one of the same gender. To enter the kingdom of God in which the Spirit shapes life according to "the will of God" is to be willing to participate in the death and resurrection of Christ. According to Herzog, the invitation to be born again is really the invitation to become Black. It is to embrace the cross of Christ as the point of departure for what it means to be in solidarity with the least of these. Jesus puts it in context for us in Matthew 25:40: inasmuch as you have done it to one of the least of these my brethren, you have done it unto me.

## Baptism as Interpretive Key

The Baptist theologian G. R. Beasley-Murray argues that the doctrine of baptism is the key that unlocks the doctrines of Christ, the Holy Spirit, the church, and the Christian life. We noted earlier that baptism in the early church was not in the triune name of "Father, Son, and Holy Spirit" but "in the name of Jesus Christ" (Acts 2:38). According to Beasley-Murray, baptism

---

38. Herzog, *Liberation Theology*, 63.

in the name of Jesus meant baptism for the sake of Jesus. "The name of the Lord Jesus was both called over the baptized (by the baptizer) and invoked by the baptized in prayer and confession (Acts 22:16 . . .)."[39] The calling of the name of Jesus, over the person being baptized, and the invocation of the name of Jesus by the person being baptized reference the role of the human and the divine in the act of baptism. Baptism is often referred to as an outward act that witnesses to an inner transformation. The invocation of the person being baptized acts as a confession of faith, as baptism is a public witness of the believer's union with Christ in burial and resurrection. Baptism is never done in private; it is always a public act and witness of the believer's participation in the life of Christ. Baptism is a witness to a new relationship between the baptized person and Christ. In a profound sense, the baptized person can now say, "Jesus is Lord." "For the Lord to whom a convert was baptized was the crucified One, raised and exalted by God to be the messianic King. However rudimentarily the Church in its earliest days may have understood it, the baptism it practiced signified that the redemption had been accomplished, the new age had dawned, and the new covenant had been made whereby it might be entered, and the Spirit had been bestowed as its first installment and pledge."[40] We are reminded here that at the very heart of baptism is the cross and resurrection of Christ. We are baptized into the death of Christ, and just as Jesus was raised by God, so does the believer walk in newness of life. According to Beasley-Murray, baptism becomes a witness to the redemption wrought by Christ in cross and resurrection. The miracle and mystery that baptism represents is that the believer through union with Christ in baptism participates in the salvific work of Christ. At the center of the baptismal act is the witness of the cross.

In Jamaica, where I was raised as a youngster, I recall at my own baptism, at age fourteen, there was a procession led by mothers of the church to the river where we believed our sins would be washed away. One mother was clothed in white and carried a cross and led the procession. The cross was

39. Beasley-Murray, *Baptism Today and Tomorrow*, 43.
40. Beasley-Murray, *Baptism Today and Tomorrow*, 44–45.

the symbol of our union and participation with the crucified Christ. We were taught that it was a symbol of God's displeasure with sin, but for us youth it was also a symbol of God's acceptance of us into the fellowship of the church and union with Christ. We were clear at baptism that redemption had taken place. It had taken place two thousand years ago but was also now taking place as we were immersed in the water. Our redemption had happened at the cross but was also happening. The cross carried by Mother Brown was a signal that our redemption involved both God and us; it was temporal and eternal at the same time. As the believer is related to the crucified and risen Christ through baptism, there becomes an acknowledgment that the old age of sin and strife and rebellion is on its way out and indeed the new age of righteousness and fellowship with Christ made possible through the gift of the Holy Spirit is on its way in. There was a profound sense that things were different; something had happened at the cross. Union with Christ through baptism had been effected. Through baptism the believer was now in union with the crucified and risen Lord.

At my baptism, all who were to be baptized were dressed in white clothes that we wore from home. We were instructed to wear something white as a symbol of purity, but the church mothers impressed on us that something was more important even than the white clothes: we were to bring a change of clothing to be placed in a booth erected on the banks of the river where we were baptized. As we came up out of the water, a church mother would lead us into the booth, where we would take off our old clothes, as a symbol that we had put off the old self, and put on new clothes, which symbolized that we had embraced a new life. Things were now different. We were now in a new and living relationship with Jesus. We had now, so to speak, put on the Lord Jesus Christ (Gal. 3:27). Beasley-Murray illuminates the Jamaican experience:

> The law of baptism is an all-or-none law. It is not a question of God hand-
> ing out a blessing to him/her who believes and is baptized, but of God
> uniting us with Christ and with Him freely giving us all things. . . . "The
> blessing that is bestowed upon the baptized man [person] does not consist
> in an individual gift of grace, nor in a particular religious condition, but in

a union with Christ, by which the totality of God's gifts are obtained. For which reason the baptismal preaching consistently uses the whole Gospel in its entirety for the interpretation of baptism."[41]

What God offers us in union with Christ is not just elements of grace or mercy but God's self. This is indeed the mystery and miracle of grace that points beyond the immediacy of the union of the believer with Christ who is now open to the fullness of the divine presence. Beasley-Murray reminds us that an eschatological horizon is the reality of the believer who participates in the death and resurrection of Christ.

> But Paul's thought embraces the future. "If we died with Christ, we believe that we shall also live with him" (Romans 6:8). It is a natural conclusion to draw, for we have been united with the Lord who by death and resurrection brought the Kingdom of God among men [humanity] and is to manifest it in the power and glory at his Return. If we have a share in his death and resurrection now, we shall have part in the power and glory of his final manifestation. Baptism therefore looks forward in hope, so surely as it looks backward in faith.[42]

The resurrection of Christ signifies a new hope that we are united with Christ in baptism, and this opens up a new future of transformation, liberation, and new humanity. If anyone is in Christ, he or she is new. Lo, the old is past, and all things have become new (2 Cor. 5:17). The new creation that the cross and resurrection make possible points to the new quality of life that takes on the principalities and powers and manifestations of slavery and bondage to self and manifestations of evil. The promise of the new creation is indeed the hope for a new earth and a new heaven that John saw coming down from heaven. The former things are passed away, and lo, all things have become new.

41. Beasley-Murray, *Baptism Today and Tomorrow*, 47; interior quotation is Adolf Schlatter, *Die Theologie des Neuen Testaments*, vol. 2 (Stuttgart, 1910), 495.
42. Beasley-Murray, *Baptism Today and Tomorrow*, 49–50.

## Baptism and Spirit

In the church of my youth in Jamaica, it was widely assumed that there was a vital and direct relationship between baptism and the Spirit. In our church culture throughout the Caribbean—and this is true also of Black churches in the United States—water was essential to baptism, as a connection was made between water and spirits. "Spirit" as it related to water was always plural because it included the spirit of ancestors. We believed that the waters that served as a conduit for the ancestors who came over from Africa as enslaved persons on boats to enforced labor on plantations were always a source of spiritual energy. The church mothers instructed us children to be sensitive to the force of the spirit that was in the water. We were told that we would meet the spirit at the river and that there would be a powerful spiritual presence in the water, and that when we came up out of the water, after being immersed, the spirit would descend on us. All of us children and many adults also testified to the presence of spiritual energy as we were raised up out of the water.

Much of this expectation by the church, and by the community that was present at the river to witness to our baptism, was shaped by the account of Jesus's baptism. It was of first importance to us that John the Baptist, who associated his baptism with water, made a connection of Jesus baptizing not with water but with the Holy Spirit and fire.

> "I baptize you with water for repentance, but one who is more powerful than I is coming after me; I am not worthy to carry his sandals. He will baptize you with the Holy Spirit and fire." . . . Then Jesus came from Galilee to John at the Jordan, to be baptized by him. John would have prevented him, saying, "I need to be baptized by you, and do you come to me?" But Jesus answered him, "Let it be so now; for it is proper for us in this way to fulfill all righteousness." Then he consented. And when Jesus had been baptized, just as he came up from the water, suddenly the heavens were opened to him and he saw the Spirit of God descending like a dove and alighting on him. And a voice from heaven said, "This is my Son, the Beloved, with whom I am well pleased." (Matt. 3:11, 13–17)

It seems clear that John's baptism was preparatory for the incoming kingdom announced by Jesus. Like Jesus, the Baptist calls on his audience to repent. According to John, God is ready to establish God's rule and reign, and a necessary precondition is repentance. The benefit of turning one's life around was that sin would be forgiven and a place for the believer would be secured in the kingdom of God, which was imminent. John the Baptist made it clear that his role was limited. There is one who comes after him who will fully put God's plan for redemption into action. "John can baptize with water; this external rite symbolizes the repentance which the person baptized has expressed. But John cannot give the spiritual power that forgiven men [persons] need, nor can he execute the judgement that must strike unrepentant lives. A Stronger One is coming to do these things. . . . To those who respond in repentance and . . . in faith, he will give the Holy Spirit."[43]

Floyd Filson calls attention to the unique role of Jesus in relation to John the Baptist. Jesus would baptize with the Holy Spirit and fire. It was as Jesus came up from the water that the Holy Spirit descended on him. Filson points out that the Spirit of God is not a passive presence. The Spirit is an active presence and power that awakens persons and equips them for the task to which God has called them. This is a profound insight for the ministry of liberation and emancipation. It is also instructive that the gift of the spirit to Christ is accompanied by fire, because fire represents the judgment of God on structures of oppression and all forms of sin that come between us and God. The Spirit equips us for the ministry of liberation and provides the power to challenge oppression in all its forms. At the baptism of Jesus there is revealed the triune presence of God. There is the voice of God from heaven. Jesus is affirmed and acknowledged as God's Beloved Son and is empowered by the Holy Spirit as he commences his ministry. It is also clear at the baptism of Jesus that "the Father approves his coming to baptism and joining with his people in preparing for the coming crisis."[44] At the baptism of Jesus the approbation of the triune God was revealed in the solidarity of

43. Floyd V. Filson, *A Commentary on the Gospel of St. Matthew* (London: Black, 1960), 66 (emphasis removed).
44. Filson, *Gospel of St. Matthew*, 69.

Jesus with oppressed humanity, and there at the river Jordan he received Spirit power for his ministry of liberation that lay ahead.

Beasley-Murray points out that some church traditions, such as Roman Catholic, Anglican, Methodist, Presbyterian, Lutheran, and others, posit a divorce between baptism and the Holy Spirit. In these church traditions baptism and confirmation are separated and the gift of the Holy Spirit is deferred from baptism to confirmation. "A persistent strain in Lutheranism and Presbyterianism, joined nowadays by the enthusiastic voice of Pentecostalism, makes a radical distinction between water baptism and Spirit baptism: the former is viewed as a sign, while the latter is believed to be the gift of God for faith alone."[45] According to Beasley-Murray, some Christians claim that baptism is the point of entry into the church, but in confirmation the Holy Spirit is poured out upon the believer. This depiction of baptism and confirmation set up as two acts has a feel of being artificial. "We recall the definition of baptism in 1 Peter iii:21: the baptism that saves is 'not a removal of dirt from the flesh but a pledge to God to maintain a good conscience.' The essential element in baptism, states the Apostle, is not the application of water to the body, but the pledge to God made at that time."[46] The issue here concerns the relationship between faith and baptism. In an often-quoted passage from Galatians, Paul states, "In Christ Jesus you are all sons [and daughters] of God through faith. For all you who were baptized to Christ have put on Christ." According to Paul, in baptism the baptized person puts on Christ; it is at baptism that one puts on Christ. At my own baptism at age fourteen, on coming up out of the water and being led to the booth by the church mother, I was able to take off the old clothes, which signified that I had now stepped into the new age of the kingdom of God, where God's reign was supreme. I was buried with Christ in baptism, and as I put on new clothes, I entered into newness of life symbolized by the resurrection of Christ.

45. Beasley-Murray, *Baptism Today and Tomorrow*, 52.
46. Beasley-Murray, *Baptism Today and Tomorrow*, 53.

But it is appropriate to ask, what of the infant who is baptized and unable to offer faith in Christ as an expression of the cross and resurrection dimensions of the faith expressed in the act of baptism? It is clear that for the infant there are two moments expressed in baptism. Family and friends stand in for the infant, and the church pledges before God and each other to nurture this child in the knowledge and admonition of God. Baptism for the infant is a sacrament of grace, where the church stands in for the child as the congregation is reminded that we all receive life as a gift of grace. Baptism of the infant is similar to the experience of birth, where life is received and offered as a gift. There was nothing we had to do at our physical birth. It was all done for us. Life was received as a gift. If the first act is a testament of grace, the second is an expression of "faith formed by grace." In the second act, confirmation, the disciple receives the fullness of the gift of the Holy Spirit. Barth lays out for us cardinal truths regarding baptism, whether infant or adult:

> The central meaning of baptism in its relation to the candidate is now at last clear. With divine certainty there is given to him for the glorifying of God in the up-building of the church of Jesus Christ, the promise that in the death and resurrection of Jesus Christ the grace of God avails for him and is directed to him; that in this happening he is also reborn; that, on the ground of this happening, even he may have assurance of the presence and work of the Holy Spirit; that even his sins are forgiven, that he is also a child of God; that the hope of eternal life is his also.[47]

Barth reminds us that baptism as a sacrament of grace is for the glorifying of God and the upbuilding of the church. Barth admonishes us of the danger of focusing on the benefits of baptism to the individual but omitting that baptism is primarily for the glory of God and the upbuilding of the church. It must be constantly mentioned that baptism is never a private happening;

47. Barth, *The Teaching of the Church*, 32.

it must always happen in the public sphere of the church, with the goal of giving glory to God. It is in this context that children are welcomed into the family of the church and discover themselves as an integral part of the family called church. This provides a context in which children come to know themselves as belonging to the family of faith and heed the admonition of Christ, "suffer the little children to come unto me." All members of the family are included in the covenant of grace.

# Salvation and Liberation

**M**uch of the exposure to Christian doctrine and theology in the Caribbean region came through the proclamation and teaching of missionaries from Europe and North America. These missionaries articulated a robust connection between politics and evangelization, while at the same time teaching and preaching in our churches and theological schools that the Gospels were not political, and there was no place for political praxis by indigenous pastors and teachers. It was clear to Caribbean people that missionaries brought their culture, their version of Christianity, and their values with them, and these values shaped their views of God, humanity, and the world. However, their values were not consonant with the search for humanity and the attempt of poor communities to engage a praxis that would give value and credence to the indigenous culture. Missionary theology sought to obfuscate and devalue the Black experience in the Caribbean. Jamaican theologian Ashley Smith states the problem clearly: "To Caribbean persons who have been merely churched 'belonging to Christendom' has little to do with the business of bringing home bread, having shelter over one's head or experiencing life as satisfying, fulfilling or meaningful. Christianity means little more than not to be 'pagan,' 'heathen' or 'uncivilized.' It has nothing to do with their perspective on what is human, what constitutes the good life or the viable or affirmative community."[1]

According to Smith, the understanding of God, humanity, and the world that missionaries brought to the Caribbean was not invested in the transformation of oppressive structures and the liberation of the social and economic conditions of poor people in search of their identity and their humanity. Missionaries who came from Europe or North America brought their culture and understanding of God and the good life with them. They

1. Ashley Smith, *Real Roots and Potted Plants* (Kingston, Jamaica: Mandeville Publishers, 1984), 10.

used the Bible as their primary authority to inculcate their way of life in the populace and provide theological arguments to disavow the Black experience as a source for talking about God, the world, and what it meant to be human. The liturgies and hymns introduced and promoted by missionary theology affirmed the status quo, notions of a White God, and the goal of a pseudo-Christian life—to become white as snow. Missionaries sought to relate their version of Christianity to the situation of suffering and alienation of Africa's children in the Caribbean. They articulated a Christianity that taught a spiritualized salvation, one that fostered a separation between salvation and liberation, as if the gospel had nothing to do with the real conditions in which people live.

## Salvation without Liberation

If the central theological problem for brothers and sisters in the United States is racism, a struggle with White privilege, then in the Caribbean it is colonialism—an acknowledgment and affirmation that whatever has value must be imported, whether in ideas, religion, or lifestyle. Colonial theology affirmed the status quo and kept Caribbean people subjugated and bound to a way of life that they perceived to be inferior. Even when colonial theology did not explicitly advocate human bondage, it was difficult for it to be the means of transformation and liberation. Colonial theology advocated salvation without liberation. Salvation without liberation was an explication of the saving gospel of Christ that emphasized deliverance from sin that did not seek the transformation of the vicious cycles of death: poverty, socioeconomic oppression, classism, and racism. Jesus is often referred to as effecting freedom from sin, death, and the law, without engaging the principalities and powers that blight the lives of God's children.

Some missionaries did see the Caribbean people as human beings made in the image of God, but they did not critically question ways in which the society was organized against poor people. For example, the village in which I lived and served while a pastor in Jamaica, and all the lands on which people lived and had household farms, were owned by a White man, who was a descendant of slave owners. Residents of the village were not allowed to make any improvements to the houses in which they lived, although many roofs leaked when it rained. One elderly woman, Mother Brackett, repaired her roof and was threatened with eviction, with no possibility of getting land in the area to build her house. This was when I intervened, went to see the court, and shared the plight of Mother Brackett. The judge understood, and Mother Brackett was allowed to remain in her house; others were able to make repairs and improve their situations. Many missionaries meant well but claimed that the gospel was not related to real-life situations: clean water, fresh air, a living wage, and owning land on which to grow produce and live. In the colonies, when victims are marginalized by unemployment and inadequate housing, the church often tells them, "The family that prays together stays together." The church ignored that families need housing, roofs need to be repaired, and people need jobs, nutrition, respect, and dignity. In the Caribbean we began to learn through reading the Bible for ourselves that salvation is about the whole person—body and soul, spiritual and material. Missionary theology often neglected the political and economic spheres as if the gospel of Christ had nothing to do with these areas of life. There was a failure in much missionary theology to relate the gospel to life; much of the gospel was related to heaven and the afterlife. This penchant to focus on the afterlife, or life after death, elicited a critique from the Rastafari community that Christians spend too much time talking about life after death and not enough time on life before death. The emphasis on the end of history did not provide a vision of what God was calling the church and the world to become in the here and now.

If Christ was not political, why then was he crucified by Rome? What would it mean for the church to join the poor, those edged out of society to its margins, in the search for justice and human dignity? Like the priest and the Levite, does the church bypass the person on the Jericho road who fell among thieves? One problem was that the community of the oppressed was encouraged with colonial theology to fight the devil and sin, while all the time leaving intact structures of oppression, poor housing, and malnourished children. Salvation was projected for an afterlife beyond the sky or for an understanding of the soul that had nothing to do with the body. Missionaries were usually aligned with the people in power, and the gospel of Christ did not question the unjust economic conditions that sentenced the poor to shanty towns without running water and electricity. Missionary theology, adorned with injustices, impeded the lives of the poor with promises of a better life in the distant future. There was no hope for the salvation and liberation of communities where people struggle with grinding poverty in the here and now. The church had not discovered a way for communities and families to be saved. We had to be saved individually.

Often we would see the missionaries basking in the Caribbean sun at expensive hotels while poor persons who served as cooks and waiters at the same hotels hardly made enough to pay bus fare to and from their place of employment. We are reminded of Leviticus 19:34: "You shall love the alien as yourself, for you were aliens in the land of Egypt: I am the LORD your God." In these contexts, oppressed persons are ushered into a culture of silence where they often hide their pain behind their smiles. God-talk in these contexts functions as a tool to keep things the way they were. The relationship between master and enslaved persons in North American and Caribbean contexts often provided a paradigm for future relationships, customs, and worldviews between the Christian church and the oppressed. The truth is, the church takes sides; it sides with the oppressor against "the least of these." The abolitionist Frederick Douglass frames the issue for us:

> But the church of this country is not only indifferent to the wrongs of the slave, it actually takes sides with the oppressor. It has made itself the bulwark of American slavery, and the shield of American slave hunters. Many of its eloquent Divines, who stand as the very lights of the church, have shamelessly given the sanction of religion and the Bible to the whole slave system. They have taught that man may, properly, be a slave; that the relation of master and slave is ordained of God; that to send back an escaped bondman to his master is clearly a duty of all the followers of the Lord Jesus Christ. . . . They strip the love of God of its beauty and leave

the throne of religion a huge, horrible, repulsive form. It is a religion for oppressors, tyrants, man stealers, and *thugs*.[2]

The missionary church took sides then, and today sides with the powerful against the weak and those who have fallen into the trap of poverty. One of the consequences of the church saving the soul while neglecting, and often ignoring, the body is that the church becomes otherworldly, and liberation from poverty and a poor sense of self-esteem is postponed for a tomorrow that never arrives. In this context, the central question that the Bible raises, "What must I do to be saved?" is understood in individualistic and privatistic terms. African ways of understanding the world as community and one's rhythm with nature are sacrificed for capitalistic understanding of the primacy of the individual. The presence of Christ among us as community is sacrificed for notions that we must come to Jesus individually. This emphasis ignored the priority of the ecclesial community and the reality that you cannot be a Christian all by yourself. To become a Christian is to follow Christ with others. In the construction of a new society and in the creation of a new humanity, we are called by the gospel of Christ to be in community and solidarity with others. Paul reminds us in 2 Corinthians 5:17 that if anyone is in Christ, he or she is a new creature. To be in Christ is a social reality. Professor Sergio Arce Martinez, formerly of Matanzas Theological Seminary in Cuba, writes: "First, there is no such thing as liberation of a single person all alone, which merits being called liberation. It simply does not exist. Either we are all liberated, or no one is liberated. Second, that the individual is never self-liberated, all alone. There are no spiritual resources within a single person all alone, no possibility of liberation, in the integral and Christian sense, within an individual. Thus, the need for a redeemer or liberator, the necessity for Christ."[3]

2. *The Life and Writings of Frederick Douglass*, vol. 11, *Pre–Civil War Decade, 1850–1860*, ed. Philip S. Foner (New York: International Publishers, 1997), 197.

3. Sergio Arce Martinez, "Evangelization and Politics from the Cuban Point of View," in *Evangelization and Politics*, ed. Sergio Arce Martinez and Oden Marichal (New York: Circus Inc., 1982), 50.

Just as you cannot be a Christian all by yourself, others are needed in the struggle to "make human life human and to keep human life human." We do not have the resources within ourselves to free ourselves from systemic evil; we need a redeemer. The sign that one has encountered the redeemer is that one is restored to the community/flock. This is the story of the good shepherd who went in search of the lone sheep that had gone astray. The signal that the lost one was redeemed and restored was that the sheep was restored to the flock. Salvation, like liberation, requires community.

Bob Marley, like Sergio Arce Martinez, sounds the same key: liberation requires a redeemer, someone outside of us. The resources of persons, despite their capabilities, are inadequate for the process and the miracle of redemption—liberation. Martinez then asks: Why then would we need a redeemer? Marley, in the poetics of liberation, counsels us in his song "Could You Be Loved":

> Don't let them fool you
> Or even try to school you. Oh no.
> . . . . . . . . . . . . . . . . . . . . . . . . . . . . . . .
> Love would never leave us alone.[4]

Through love, God is reconciling the world to God's self.

Marley reminds us of the priority of the Black experience in construction of a theology that has relevance for the Caribbean context. Earlier I alluded to the one symptom of an irrelevant theology—that it did not emerge from Caribbean soil but came ready-made from Europe or North America. The Caribbean theologian William Watty points to a problem that contributed to the God-talk being articulated by missionaries as irrelevant.

Watty indicates that missionaries to the Caribbean thought they had a universal theology that was applicable for all settings, including the Caribbean populace. Missionaries were convinced that they did not have anything

---

4. Bob Marley and the Wailers, "Could You Be Loved," in *Uprising* (Tuff Gong/Island, 1980).

to learn from the indigenous culture and people. The gospel of Christ was presented as a potted plant and never translated into the soil of the people. Missionaries would argue that there was no reality of a Caribbean church or Caribbean theology. There was just the church, and there was just theology. And for some time we believed them. We would sing hymns from the hymnal they brought with them about "the Negro in his blindness bows down to wood and stone." In the Baptist church I attended, in which the majority of the membership could neither read nor write in the English language, we chanted every Sunday the Te Deum Laudamus, a canticle the congregation had memorized. Like parrots, we repeated words that came from a hymnal sent from England to provide language for our invocation and praise to God. Our native language, like our instruments of praise, the banjo and drums, was not acceptable in the house of worship. We wondered if we were good enough to compose our own songs and liturgies for use in the house of God. Professor Watty states the problem: "One of the commonest ways in which theology has and can still become prone to unreality is by the spurious claim to universality and finality. If it is true that we know only in part and we see through a glass darkly, then every brand of theology must necessarily be limited and every theological formulation partial and provisional. In other words, there is no theology so far formulated which has not been contextual. . . . And what is this universal theology but European or Western Theology? This is, in fact, the theology which we received."[5]

Watty reminds us that all theology is contextual and that we had appropriated European and American worldviews about God, ourselves, and the world. According to Watty, the worlds from which we received notions about God, Christ, and salvation also gave us New World slavery, racism, militarism, and the genocide of the Arawaks and Caribs (Indian populations in the Caribbean). Theology came as a form of colonial exploitation. Perhaps an important index of our liberation and salvation was the discovery that God was neither European nor American. Perhaps it is as Frantz Fanon, who

---

5. William Watty, *From Shore to Shore: Soundings in Caribbean Theology* (Kingston, Jamaica: UTCWI Press, 1981), 3.

hails from the Caribbean, informed us, that Caribbean theology begins with the good news from the Gospel of Matthew: "The last will be first, and the first will be last" (20:16). The new knowledge we learned was that although our received and embedded theologies were from Europe and the United States, the Bible was uniquely our book, the Bible of our ancestors. Our approach to theology was pragmatic. We took from missionary theology whatever we found helpful for the journey toward liberation and salvation. Caribbean people began to read the Bible for themselves in the context of the search for freedom and emancipation. It was this rereading of the Bible for ourselves that rekindled our hope in a new future as revivalist, Rastafari, and Afro-Pentecostal expressions of faith took center stage.

It is interesting that what has separated Caribbean expressions of the faith from non-Caribbean expressions is a profound dependence on the authority of the Bible, and a keen sense that the Bible is the people's book. An interesting index of the faith in the authority of the Bible was that Caribbean people read the Scriptures in the light of the struggle of poor people to make sense of their existence in a culture rife with epistemic violence. Their interpretation of the Bible in the light of their oppressed condition was not dependent on their ability to read the book. Often, at religious ceremonies at the market square, or in the open air under a tree, a child, or young initiate, would be called on to read. Although the leader could not read, she would tell the reader where to read, and if the reader erred, the illiterate leader would correct her. Caribbean people had memorized the Bible just as they had memorized the Te Deum Laudamus. As Caribbean people begin to re-read the Bible in the light of "the preferential option for the poor," texts that were often on their lips were:

> Thus says the LORD: Do not let the wise boast in their wisdom, do not let the mighty boast in their might, do not let the wealthy boast in their wealth; but let those who boast boast in this, that they understand and know me, that I am the LORD; I act with steadfast love, justice, and righteousness in the earth; for in these things I delight, says the LORD. (Jer. 9:23–24)

But God chose what is foolish in the world to shame the wise; God chose what is weak in the world to shame the strong; God chose what is low and despised in the world, things that are not, to reduce to nothing things that are, so that no one might boast in the presence of God. (1 Cor. 1:27–29)

## Becoming Black with Christ

The good news is for the poor, "those who have left their nets" to follow Jesus. The poor are those who have given up everything in discipleship to Jesus. To be among the poor is to become Black with Christ. To become Black with Christ is to enter into solidarity with the poor and to see in their suffering the suffering of God. The cross of Christ is not just the passion narrative of Christ that occurred two thousand years ago, but the recognition of the suffering of the poor as God's suffering. "The interpretation of Jesus' suffering in the light of Isaiah's Suffering Servant situates the cross on the side of the poor and afflicted, the sick and the oppressed. Such contextualization is carried even further in Paul's linkage of the cross with the incarnation. According to Paul, Jesus took the form of a slave in his incarnation, becoming totally identified with humanity in its lowest form. The cross is the ultimate test of this identification: Jesus became obedient unto death (Phil. 2:8)."[6] Orlando Costas reminds us that Jesus was a Jew, and the Jewishness of Jesus gives us permission to talk about and acknowledge God's delight in the ethnicity and particularity of our humanity. The God who is revealed in Jesus is not a stranger to those who are despised and rejected. In fact, the humanity of Christ forces us to ask, in the language of Dietrich Bonhoeffer, "what form does Christ take in the world today?" Here is one answer Caribbean Christians attribute to Jesus:

> He was despised and rejected by others;
> a man of suffering and acquainted with infirmity;

6. Orlando E. Costas, *Christ outside the Gate* (Maryknoll, NY: Orbis Books, 1995), 7.

> and as one from whom others hid their faces
>> he was despised, and we held him of no account.
> Surely he has borne our infirmities
>> and carried our diseases;
> yet we accounted him stricken,
>> struck down by God and afflicted.
> But he was wounded for our transgressions,
>> crushed for our iniquities;
> upon him was the punishment that made us whole,
>> and by his bruises we are healed. (Isa. 53:3–5)

The main point here is that Jesus cast his lot with the poor. What form does Christ take in the world today? Christ takes on the form of the Black community. To be Black is to be despised and rejected. However, we should not miss that this is the way to salvation. The suffering of the poor, those who are not desired, the forsaken ones, becomes the pathway to salvation and new life. Unless one becomes Black, that is, takes on the Black condition and enters into solidarity with the oppressed, those who are despised and rejected, one will not inherit the kingdom of God. Christ is among us as the forsaken one. The theological imperative is that for a community to be saved it must come through the door of blackness. The call to blackness is inseparable from the call of God because God manifest in Jesus is inseparable from the community of the poor. There is a temptation to dislodge the cross of Christ from "the hermeneutical privilege" of the Black experience and place it in neutral ground where the oppressor may access it without reference to the oppressed. Scripture makes it clear that the cross of Christ is inseparable from the community of the oppressed. This is the theological import of Matthew 25:35, "For I was hungry and you gave me food, I was thirsty and you gave me something to drink, I was a stranger and you welcomed me." Scripture and church tradition remind us that Jesus died on a cross "not between two candles, but between two thieves." He was abandoned by his closest friends, was sold for thirty pieces of silver, and was buried in a borrowed grave. "This is carried a step further in Hebrews 13:13 where Jesus' death is located 'outside' the Holy City—the place where the leftovers of the cultic sacrifices were thrown. . . . The fact that the community of faith is to go to him 'outside the camp' and 'bear the abuse he endured' indicates that for the writer of Hebrews the risen Lord is to be located in the battles and heat of history, among the nonpersons of society."[7]

At the very center of Black theology is a struggle with the cross of the Black experience. In most of the Caribbean islands Black is not beautiful. There is an element of the tragic and the grotesque associated with the cross of the Black experience, as Caribbean people adorn the cross with flowers. The cross of the Black experience has often been a stumbling block for middle-class Christians who seek to leave the poor behind and embrace the world of capitalism and consumerism. One reality is that we are enchanted by materialism; we believe that life consists in what we have or possess. This zeal to possess, to have more, alienates us from our true selves, others, and God. This passion to possess often separates us from others and our environment. We begin to identify ourselves as competitors and consumers. We forget that we are called to love and to reconciliation; we sin against the neighbor. Our gaze wanders from the one who gave us life and called us into being. One aspect of what it means to be human is to remember that our life is a gift from God and that God has placed us on earth to care for creation, to be there for others and thereby discover our connectedness with creation, others, and God. To forget the alien and the stranger is to forget that we were also aliens and strangers in "Egypt." When we talk about what is wrong with us, we at the same time acknowledge what is right with us. What is right with us is that the God who calls us into covenant is among us as friend and advocate. God reaffirms God's covenant with us. Caribbean theologian Hyacinth Boothe writes:

> In the Jamaican situation the European stance toward "*negritude*" [the perception that there is an ontological built-in inferiority in the racial physical features of Africans] has been a determinant in social niche, economic

7. Costas, *Christ outside the Gate*, 7.

status, and the sense of personal worth. . . . The church has contributed to the resulting self-hate experienced by so many people. This experience is not peculiar to Jamaica and the Caribbean. In the mid-twentieth century, Rosa Parks initiated the movement in which Martin Luther King, succeeded by such persons as Jesse Jackson, sought in various ways to challenge Afro-Americans to develop a personal consciousness of "*somebodiness.*" These persons were influenced by the Jamaican, Marcus Garvey. In Jamaica, within the context of the Church, Garvey had come to the realization that his black color was conceived to confer upon him the status of unconditional and perpetual inferiority in the midst of a population that was predominantly black, and so he set out on a personal crusade to redeem the black race and to establish the fact of the human integrity and racial equality of the African.[8]

Hyacinth Boothe argues that perhaps no other place in the world has been subjected to the onslaught of colonial culture as the Caribbean. The European began in the Caribbean with Christopher Columbus in 1492 and continues to this day, although a number of countries gained their independence in the 1960s, except for Haiti, which became an independent state in 1804. One of the consequences of the sustained power of European presence in these Caribbean nation-states is what Boothe refers to as "*the white bias.*" According to Professor Boothe, the gospel of Jesus Christ needs to be set free from the racial and cultural entrapment that holds it in bondage. It must declare the saving activity of God expressed in Jesus Christ for victims everywhere. Barriers must be broken down so that Caribbean families may live in justice and peace. Boothe relates the gospel of Christ to political and religious oppression.

God's liberation of the children of Israel from political and religious bondage reaffirms the need for a new exodus of Caribbean people and Black people in the New World who are in need of socioeconomic and religious liberation. Exodus 20:2, "I am the LORD your God, who brought you out of the land of

8. Hyacinth I. Boothe, "A Theological Journey for an Emancipatory Theology," *Caribbean Journal of Religious Studies* 17, no. 1 (April 1996): 17.

Egypt, out of the house of slavery." Caribbean people have always been inspired by the biblical exodus story and have seen this liberation as the main key in which liberation is set. With exploitation and poverty as a cultural backdrop, Caribbean people dream of a new exodus, one that would address the history of slavery and oppression and offer a vision of a new humanity.

In his exodus song, Bob Marley wails that Jah (God) would send us another brother Moses because "we gonna cross the Red Sea." The call for another brother Moses may have been a dream that someone in the tradition of Marcus Garvey would lead us out of poverty and the manifold expressions of exploitation that plague the Caribbean. Marley understood that life in the Caribbean was for the oppressed poor one of economic and often political violence. Leadership out of Babylon had to come from Jah (God), and so he wailed like the biblical prophets in the Old Testament:

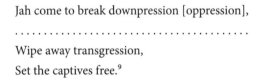

> Jah come to break downpression [oppression],
> . . . . . . . . . . . . . . . . . . . . . . . . . . . . . . . . . . . . .
> Wipe away transgression,
> Set the captives free.[9]

Help for redemption and liberation had to come not from human hands but from the divine. With the song, which is beyond the reach of the oppressor, Marley, in the tradition of another "brother Moses," awakens the poor and exploited persons in the Caribbean and urges them: "Get up and stand up for your rights." Poor people became keenly aware of their situation, and Marley wails, "Are you satisfied with the life you are living?" Through music there was a call to consciousness that exploded on the airwaves, and the poor were informed and instructed that they were no longer "nobodies" but were now armed with "redemption songs," which were songs of freedom. With dreams of a new exodus and armed with these songs of freedom, the poor and dispossessed were encouraged to become agents of their own liberation. Jah

9. Bob Marley and the Wailers, "Exodus," in *Exodus* (Tuff Gong/Island, 1977); see *The Complete Lyrics of Bob Marley: Songs of Freedom*, ed. Harry Hawke (London: Omnibus, 2001), 48–49.

(God) is on the side of those who weep and are victimized. Jah is the one who stands up for the weak and all who are disabled. In Kingston, Jamaica, where Marley lived each day, he would see hundreds of women who could find no employment and many who were landless and homeless. As far as Babylon (capitalism) was concerned, these people do not exist. Marley wails as he offers hope to the poor and forsaken, "Jah have we for a purpose and a reason." Marley challenges the poor and hopeless to rediscover the purpose and the reason Jah created them in the first place. What is at stake is the liberating agency of the divine expressed in the community of the exploited and oppressed.

Barbara Makeda Blake Hannah captures the spirit of the new exodus from "nobodiness" to "somebodiness" as she explains:

> Like Garvey before him, Bob helped us free ourselves from those pains and replace them with the joys of being a part of a New Creation of Black Madonnas, of a new African-ness, cleansed with a new vision, a wider breadth and richer strength. That vision encompassed a view of a Black warrior, bearing not a spear or a gun, but the peaceful music of Love – Love of Black Man, Love of Black Woman, Love of Black People and Love of All people.[10]

The song becomes a strategy for liberation as it transforms us; we deconstruct language and reality as we refuse to be made in another's image. To become somebody, we do not have to be somebody else.

## Toward a New Exodus

We noted earlier that a working definition of Black theology is Black people reflecting on their place in history and agitating to change the world in the confidence that the God revealed in Scripture as creator, redeemer, and

10. Barbara Makeda Blake Hannah, *Rastafari: The New Creation*, 4th ed. (Kingston, Jamaica: Masquel, 1997), 54.

sustainer empowers them in that struggle. The goal of Black theology is a new exodus and the emergence of a new creation; it is the transformation of society in keeping with a trinity of values: justice, hope, and love. In the language of Caribbean theologians, theology must be in harmony with God's will to set at liberty all who are captives.

The Bible has great significance to the church and to communities outside the church such as Rastafarians, who also base their theological assumptions on the Bible. If in the Old Testament there are illustrations of God freeing a particular people from slavery and oppression, in the New Testament this liberating activity has meaning on a universal level. In the New Testament, the saving activity of God is made available to the outsider and the nonperson. And this articulates an approach to method in theology, in that the divine activity is not only seen in particular communities such as the children of Israel but, in the New Testament, is made available to all humanity through the incarnation and resurrection of Christ. Scripture seems to teach us that in the incarnation God became Black. Orlando Costas captures Scripture's witness to the identification of Christ with the least of these.

> He was a Jew, the son of a modest family, who grew up in an insignificant town in the province farthest from the capital and the most culturally backward. He spoke with a Galilean accent, had a limited formal education, and was a carpenter by trade. He was aware that he belonged to a "unique people, although one humiliated for centuries by foreigners." Yet he was misunderstood by his family, his friends, his disciples, and the religious leaders of his country. From the time he left home to become an itinerant preacher, he lived a poor and lonely life with no permanent abode. He so identified himself with the poor and the oppressed that he dedicated himself to a suffering service in their behalf.[11]

If the Jewishness of Jesus grants us permission to talk about the social location of the poor, the resurrection of the crucified one also mandates

11. Costas, *Christ outside the Gate*, 6.

that Jesus belongs to the poor in all places. Students in theological schools would remind us that this is another way to talk about cross and resurrection, or the humanity and divinity of Jesus Christ. If on the one hand the humanity of Jesus points to his solidarity with the poor and afflicted, on the other hand the divinity of Christ points to his saving power to overcome suffering and death. This double foci has special meaning for communities of the poor in bondage to poverty or illness of the mind or body. It is their confidence that through the power of the resurrection, Christ overcomes the vicious forces of death and alienation. To give a testimony that Jesus lives, as we do in Caribbean and in African American churches, is to share the confidence that death, disease, and poverty do not have the last word. As we often say in Black churches, whether in the Caribbean or in the United States, "Christ took on death in order to overcome death." This means that the poor are not scared of suffering but, like Jesus, take it on either by necessity or by choice in order to overcome it. This means that suffering does not become the last word but points as a pathway to resurrection. Christ is our hope; the power of his presence in suffering indicates that suffering is not the last word. Through the cross of Christ, God identifies with all who have been set aside by society, takes their burdens upon the divine self, and overcomes them not merely for the poor of the Jewish nation but for the poor everywhere. In Christ God becomes one of the poor, and it is the embodiment of Christ, God's Son, that is the point of departure for how the poor understand themselves. The mystery of the cross is that God in his Son Jesus Christ is now numbered with the poor. We have been saying that in Jesus we can look back, on the one hand, to God's history with Israel as a particular community in which the liberating activity of God among victims of oppression was made plain, and on the other hand, we look forward to God's promises to be with all God's children who are held in captivity. This means that the captives who are enslaved by oppression and bondage are not without hope, because the Christ who is among them as friend and savior is their hope for a new exodus from traditions that enslave and disable them into a new humanity made possible by the Christ who offers healing and salvation.

Paul stumbled on the new exodus and new humanity made possible in the presence of Christ among his people. "There is no longer Jew or Greek, there is no longer slave or free, there is no longer male and female; for all of you are one in Christ Jesus" (Gal. 3:28). Brad Braxton helps us understand that in this wonderful breakthrough we should guard against notions of a forced unity that dispenses with ethnicity. Paul, according to Braxton, is not obliterating difference in stating that we are neither Jew nor Greek, slave nor free, male and female, but Paul warns us against the embrace of dominance. Braxton illuminates the Pauline context:

> Some interpreters have referred to Paul's words in 3:28 as the "Magna Carta" of the New Testament. This declaration affirms that Christ has liberated believers not from the tyranny of difference but from the tyranny of sameness. The particular domination visited upon the Gentiles in Galatia was the coercion for them to be Jews. Quests for unity that presuppose or even demand sameness misconstrue Paul's dynamic, expansive notion of Christian unity. Our unity in Christ does not consist of an amalgamated or undifferentiated identity. Rather we are "one in Christ" because each Christian individual and each Christian community has a relationship in faith with Christ, and these faith (ful) relationships with Christ are meant to ensure that we relate to each other, in the midst of our many differences, with mutuality and equality.[12]

Braxton reminds us that it is faith in Christ that sets us apart as children of God. As God's children, we have access to the tree of life and our full participation in the covenant of grace is assured. When Paul uses the phrase "in Christ Jesus" in Galatians 3:26 and elsewhere, he is pointing to the social and ethical understanding of communal life under the Lordship of Christ. According to Braxton, in Galatians 3:28 Paul underscores three areas of challenge to the church in Galatia: (1) the ethnic challenge ("there is no longer

---

12. Brad Ronnell Braxton, *No Longer Slaves: Galatians and African American Experience* (Collegeville, MN: Liturgical Press, 2002), 94–95.

Jew or Greek"), (2) the challenge of social class ("there is no longer slave or free"), and (3) gender relationships ("there is no longer male and female"). The emphasis in this epistle and perhaps the reason Paul wrote is to clarify that gentiles do not have to become Jews in order to participate in the full benefits of the covenant of grace. Paul is not instructing the congregation at Galatia how they should live in the eschaton. The emphasis is on a crisis in the church in Galatia, and it is an attempt of Paul to relate faith and life in the social settings in which the members of this church find themselves. Congregational harmony is similar to the harmony when the black and white keys of the piano are engaged. It is the distinctiveness of each that provides the harmony and melody that makes a profound difference. There is no need for Jews and Greeks to blend in and lose their distinctiveness. Unity does not mean uniformity. Braxton helps us celebrate a God who created a world that is different certainly from the creator and in which God delights in the differences among us. It has often been pointed out that God in Christ Jesus did not become a universal person, but Christ came among us and lived among us a Jew, and the Jewishness of Jesus gives us permission to celebrate our own ethnicities. Braxton amplifies this perspective: "Christ has freed the African American to say, 'yes' to blackness. Historically, our blackness has been despised. Now under a specious artificial unity being promoted in certain circles our blackness may be ignored. All Americans (and certainly all Christians) should strive for unity, but genuine unity will emerge from a dialogue among culturally distinct groups. . . . If racial unity is to be brought to life in America, white Americans will have to experience the birth pangs of confronting and dealing with, not ignoring, or obliterating the 'otherness' of our blackness."[13]

I am grateful to Braxton for sounding the key of harmony and unity yet affirming otherness in his attempt to talk about reconciliation that does not obfuscate difference. One emphasis that Braxton highlights is that harmony, unity, and reconciliation as goals for our communal life must acknowledge the process of liberation. An important key for Braxton is that if God in

13. Braxton, *No Longer Slaves*, 95–96.

Christ is reconciling the world unto God's self, artificial unity and social arrangements that promote the dominance of one group over another are abolished. Perhaps we should begin to think of equality as a gift of the spirit of God, since reconciliation presupposes equality, a new exodus from what Braxton calls "specious artificial unity" in which dispositions of weakness and accommodation of those without power create injury to those willing to sacrifice justice for peace. A peace that will last must meet the test of justice being done. To say yes to blackness means that the poor and those who suffer because of injustice must be willing to say no to those who would deny total liberation. In Christ, a new center of value emerges and master-slave ways of relating and understanding the world are abolished. There is no longer a value gap among rich and poor; our identity is now in Christ Jesus.

The challenge that Braxton raises for Black theology is for us to begin to ask what liberation would mean not just among us as individuals but between classes. This is especially poignant in the Caribbean, where crossing class differences is more problematic than navigating racial lines. What would liberation mean in a place where persons do not meet and communicate across class and social differences? What does it mean to be saved in this context? I do not believe Braxton's exposition at this level is helpful; he sees dialogue as a strategy of liberation. It is at this level that we have to remember the liberating activity of the divine on behalf of those held captive by those who wield power over the powerless. We must ask what it means to do God's will in situations in which the poor have to confront power wielded by the state and by institutions.

In recent times, no one has taken on the socioeconomic dimensions of class oppression and the challenge among classes to make the promise of democracy a reality like Martin Luther King Jr. King's essential challenge to us was that of a praxis-oriented theologian who engaged theological issues from which to create the Beloved Community. The Beloved Community was King's attempt to do theology from within the struggle to eke out a measure of dignity and self-respect for the exploited and victimized. King works from within the struggle: "But when you have seen vicious mobs lynch your mothers and fathers at will and drown your sisters and brothers at whim; when you have seen hate filled policemen curse, kick and even kill your black brothers and sisters; when you see the vast majority of your twenty million Negro brothers smothering in an airtight cage of poverty in the midst of an affluent society."[14]

James Cone, who regarded Martin Luther King Jr. as one of his theological mentors, states the theological priority of praxis:

> To preach the gospel today means confronting the world with the reality of human freedom. It means telling black people that their slavery has come to an end and telling whites to let go of the chains. Black people do not have to live according to white rules. If the gospel is "the power of God unto salvation," then black people have a higher loyalty to him that cuts across every sphere of human existence. Preaching the gospel is nothing but proclaiming to blacks that they do not have to submit to ghetto-existence. Our new existence has been bought and paid for; we are now redeemed, set free. Now it is incumbent upon us to behave as free persons.[15]

An important theme Braxton highlighted in his exegesis of Paul's discussion of the relationship of gentile and Jew in the churches of Galatia was that gentiles do not have to pattern or imitate Jews in order to be heirs of the freedom made possible by the Christ event. The Christ event was transformative: "For in Christ Jesus you are all children of God through faith" (Gal. 3:26). Gentiles are also the children of God, and as such they participate in all the blessings of the covenant community. Both King and Cone agree with Braxton that there is no need to posit a "raceless," nameless, or faceless humanity. King and Cone were committed to practicing theology from within the struggle. They sought to change the oppressive situation that stymied the prospects of the poor affirming their humanity as children of God. As good theologians, liberation and reconciliation provided revolutionary principles

14. Martin Luther King Jr., *Why We Can't Wait* (New York: New American Library, 1963), 86.

15. James H. Cone, *A Black Theology of Liberation* (Philadelphia: Lippincott, 1970), 231.

that helped to question oppression in a theological way. The critical question that King and Cone help us with is how theology becomes revolutionary activity. Both King and Cone began with the priority of God being at work in the world, overturning traditions and practices that blight and hold in captivity the dreams and hopes of God's children agitating for liberation and reconciliation. King, who not only gave us revolutionary principles to help change the face of society but offered up in the service of democracy a revolutionary life as an oblation, states: "Today we know with certainty that segregation is dead. . . . When in future generations men look back upon these turbulent, tension packed days through which we are passing, they will see God working through history for the salvation of man [humanity]. They will know that God was working through these men [human beings] who had the vision to perceive that no nation could survive half slave and half free. God is able to conquer the evils of history."[16] According to Cone, the pre–Civil War Black church influenced Martin Luther King Jr., allowing him to advocate breaking unjust laws. The pre–Civil War ministers of the Black church were willing to fight the system of slavery until death. According to Cone, the pre–Civil War Black church provided the inspiration for King to institute a program of civil disobedience. Cone calls attention to the debt the Black church as a whole owes King:

> At least during the early stages of this movement was a return to the spirit of the pre–Civil War black preachers with the emphasis being on freedom and equality in the present political structure. King saw clearly the meaning of the gospel with its social implications and sought to instill its true spirit in the hearts and minds of black and white in this land. He was a man endowed with a charisma of God; he was a prophet in our own time. And like no other black or white American he could set black people's hearts on fire with the gospel of freedom in Christ which would make them willing to give up all for the sake of black humanity.[17]

16. Martin Luther King Jr., *Strength to Love* (Cleveland: Collins, 1963), 110.
17. James H. Cone, *Black Theology and Black Power* (New York: Seabury, 1969), 108.

Cone admits that King was not comfortable with the notion of Black power and would have had difficulties with the notion of Black theology. Yet, according to Cone, King's vision was the inspiration for Black power and Black theology in the attempt to make King's dream a reality. However, once we get beyond labels of Black theology and Black power, there are striking similarities between the approaches of Cone and King. Both theologians seek to relate the gospel of Jesus Christ to the existential situation in which the poor and afflicted search for meaning and fulfillment as daughters and sons of God. It is also fair to state that both assert a christological focus in their attempt to relate the gospel to the situation in which the poor are humiliated.

The way forward is to struggle against and break the chains that bind the poor and oppressed as they announce that in Christ Jesus salvation and liberation are conjoined. In Galatians 5:1, Paul declares, "For freedom Christ has set us free." Freedom is the will and ability to struggle against all that would encroach against one's call and vocation to be human. The conjoining of salvation and liberation is a reminder that the good news that the gospel of Christ declares is not only for a changed person but also for changed circumstances. The gospel must announce that change is required in the socioeconomic and sociological situation. It is not enough to rescue the person who was robbed on the Jericho road. The conditions on that road need to be changed, so that the dangers that threaten human well-being are removed. When the church asks for a changed person and not a changed situation in which that person lives, the church fails to help create conditions for human flourishing and denies the creation of conditions for human freedom. Freedom should not be separated from hope. God's children need to dream a new tomorrow, a new world, and a new church, one discontinuous from the yesterdays of marginalization and self-defacement. Hope reminds us that freedom is not merely an idea in the future but is a liberation project in the present. Hope is the vision of a new heaven and a new earth that is actualized in the present.

The Christian has to live with two warrants at once. Salvation must mean at the same time a commitment for structural change and personal transformation. The person who has discovered God's will for her life cannot any longer live as a detached observer of history but must begin to agitate and rebel to change the world. Hope provides a vision of what the world may become. It is of first importance to be reminded that God, who is revealed in Jesus Christ, although not limited to history, is present in history as savior, friend, and hope. Whenever the church forgets this, it calls people to its ways and not to God's ways. Hope that is grounded in the freedom of God becomes a critique of society, as "the blind receive their sight, the lame walk, the lepers are cleansed, the deaf hear, the dead are raised, and the poor have good news preached to them" (Matt. 11:5; cf. Luke 4:18). The good news, then, is the summons to freedom, where God reigns and victims are set free for freedom.

Although hope has a "not yet" quality, because of the possibility for hope to be incarnate in history and provide a glimpse of what the world may become, oppressed people begin to agitate to change the world. This means then that changing the structures of oppression and changing the individual are not two separate events but two aspects of the same event. Cone captures the double foci that is at the heart of salvation and liberation:

> Because God has set us free, we are now commanded to go and be reconciled with our neighbors, and particularly our white neighbors. But this does not mean letting whites define the terms of reconciliation. It means participating in God's revolutionizing activity in the world, changing the political, economic, and social structures so that distinctions between rich and poor, oppressed and oppressors, are no longer a reality. To be reconciled to white people means destroying their oppressive power, reducing them to the human level and thereby putting them on an equal footing with other humans. There can be no reconciliation with masters as long as they are masters, as long as men are in prison. . . . The Christian task is to rebel against all masters, destroying their pretensions to authority and ridiculing the symbols of power.[18]

18. James H. Cone, *Risks of Faith: The Emergence of a Black Theology of Liberation, 1968–1998* (Boston: Beacon, 1999), 39.

Cone reminds us that sin not only is an act of individuals but also has corporate and structural dimensions. Sin is not merely a private and individualistic transgression that may be atoned for by an individual act of confession, which leaves unchallenged the social order in which persons without power are set aside and placed on reservations or in prisons. Salvation and liberation must come to grips with sin that expresses itself in social, historical forms of exploitation and domination of peoples, races, and classes. Paul hints in this direction when he speaks of evil as "principalities and powers." Sin builds up corporate structures of alienation and oppression that a person cannot overcome by an act of confession. Salvation from corporate evil may mean that the community must participate in political processes that seek to root out structures that diminish and blight the lives of God's children. Therefore, a part of what it means to be a disciple is to belong to a community and tradition that are on the one hand objective to the individual and on the other hand formative to the individual's new life. A faith relationship with Christ does not allow one to become a private disciple who refuses to identify and participate in the life of the community.

This means, among other things, that the disciple cannot merely ask, "What am I to believe?" but must at the same time ask, "What am I to do?" In other words, orthodoxy—correct belief or beliefs—must not be separated from orthopraxis—correct action. With 1 John, we must affirm that to know the truth is to do the truth. Faith in Christ should not be reduced to getting right information in terms of learning correct doctrines, but rather faith is fidelity. What is needed here is a hermeneutic of trust: "This is his commandment, that we should believe in the name of his Son Jesus Christ and love one another, just as he has commanded us. All who obey his commandments abide in him, and he abides in them" (1 John 3:23–24). It seems that John's opponents were claiming to know God (2:4), but John inquires: What is the test of knowing God? How may we be sure that we know God? For John the test is fidelity. It is in the act of fidelity that the disciple is assured that the love of God is at work in him or her and in the community.

The conjoining of the questions "What am I to believe?" and "What am I to do?" helps to join faith and praxis together. Two readings from the Old Testament indicate God as the content of faith:

> Yet I have been the LORD your God
>> ever since the land of Egypt;
> you know no God but me,
>> and besides me there is no savior. (Hos. 13:4)

> I am the LORD your God, who brought you out of the land of Egypt, out of the house of slavery; you shall have no other gods before me. (Exod. 20:2–3)

It begins to become clear that there is an exodus principle in much of the Old Testament. Yahweh continually reminds Israel of their deliverance from the house of bondage. The exodus principle becomes a principle of faith. "Faith means leaving Egypt." Faith means joining God in God's work in the world on behalf of widows and orphans.

> You shall not abuse any widow or orphan. If you do abuse them, when they cry out to me, I will surely heed their cry; my wrath will burn, and I will kill you with the sword. (Exod. 22:22–24)

> He has told you, O mortal, what is good;
>> and what does the LORD require of you
> but to do justice, and to love kindness,
>> and to walk humbly with your God? (Mic. 6:8)

The theme of a God who is made known through suffering runs through Scripture and the Christian tradition. In Philippians 2:5 we are instructed that the form Christ takes in the world is that of a servant. To be formed with Christ is to join in solidarity with Christ and to offer our lives in service for others (Mark 10:45). As we enter into solidarity with victims and those who are told to stay in their place, we exit traditions of domination and hierarchy as we announce that, because of the presence of the crucified and risen one among us, change is already taking place as poverty and questions of identity do not have the final word. And this is what faith must mean in the context of extreme oppression: that the present order of injustice is on its way out. The night of oppression and pain is on its way out, and the dawn of the abundant life, faith, hope, and justice is at hand. Faith means leaving the house of bondage and saying no to all forces that impinge on the freedom to embrace our new identity as daughters and sons of the Most High. We are clear concerning the divine activity on behalf of all who are of low degree: "He has scattered the proud in the imagination of their hearts, he has put down the mighty from their thrones, and exalted those of low degree. . . . God is at work, to pluck up and break down, to destroy and to overthrow, to build and to plant. For behold a king is born in the city of David, a savior who is Christ the Lord . . . a babe wrapped in swaddling clothes and lying in a manger. Behold, this child is set for the falling and rising of many in Israel."[19]

19. This mixture of texts was arranged by Paul Lehmann, *Ethics in a Christian Context* (New York: Harper & Row, 1976), 99.

# Christology and Grace in Womanist Thinking

Contemporary expressions of womanist theology have their anteced-ents in Black theology. Several womanist thinkers, Delores Williams, Jacquelyn Grant, Katie Cannon, and Kelly Brown Douglas, received their doctor of philosophy degrees at Union Theological Seminary, in New York, and pursued much of their graduate studies with Prof. James Cone. Because these scholars were thought leaders in the articulation and development of womanist thinking, it is surprising that in the first decade of the development of Black theology, Cone did not accord womanist thinkers the same visibility that he granted male scholars in his first book, *Black Theology and Black Power*, and especially in *Black Theology: A Documentary History, 1966–1979*, coedited with Gayraud Wilmore. Commenting on the marginalization of womanist scholars in this text, Wilmore offers his opinion:

> Part V, we willingly concede, is something of an embarrassment. Why should essays written by Black women be consigned to a separate section? The articles themselves, introduced by James Cone, who has experienced the burden of representing the men before conferences of Black women theological students, defines the problem. Black theology has been a Black-male-dominated enterprise and to the extent that it continues to be so, our sisters say quite clearly, it cannot be an authentic means of liberation.
>
> The overwhelming predominance of Black women in our churches makes the situation all the more ironical.[1]

The question raised acknowledges relegating the voices of Black women to section 5 of a documentary history and raises serious questions con-cerning the invisibility of women in Black theology. This is brought to the

---

1. Gayraud Wilmore and James Cone, eds., *Black Theology: A Documentary History, 1966–1979* (Maryknoll, NY: Orbis Books, 1979), 7.

fore in Cone's first book, *Black Theology and Black Power*, in which Cone betrays a commitment to White ways of thinking about Christ, humanity, and the world. Cone engages White thinkers as diverse as Emil Brunner, Rudolf Bultmann, Dietrich Bonhoeffer, Billy Graham, Karl Barth, and Reinhold Niebuhr. Cone was introduced to White ways of thinking in seminary and graduate school, where he wrote a dissertation on Karl Barth's anthropology.

Cone said a primary reason for his articulation of Black theology was the exclusion of Black ways of thinking by White religionists. In part 3 of *Black Theology: A Documentary History, 1966–1979*, Cone allots much space to Paul Lehmann, Helmut Gollwitzer, John Bennett, Paul Holmer, G. Clark Chapman, and David J. Bosch. Why assign chapters to White theologians in a book on Black theology? Do Cone and Wilmore embrace the stranger and thereby openly support a cardinal tenet of Black ecclesiology that affirms the insistence of the practice of love in the Black church? Wilmore acknowledged that in turning to the stranger—a tenet of Black church hospitality— Black theology unwittingly affirmed the invisibility and marginality of Black women. Black women were excluded and had to wait their turn at the back of the line, so to speak. "Could it be that because Black women were of the same race, culture and in many instances religion, they were excluded? Was sameness a problem? Did black theologians fail to note that sameness does not mean identical? While Black theologians saw white men as different and understood difference in terms of transcendence, they understood black women in terms of the familiar and overlooked issues of transcendence."[2]

Cone acknowledged the habit and prerogative of Black men to speak on behalf of and for Black women and noted that this was one way to diminish and demean women. Cone frames the issue:

The most glaring limitation of *A Black Theology of Liberation* was my failure to be receptive to the problem of sexism in the black community and

2. Noel Leo Erskine, "Light from Black Theology," in *Sources of Light: Resources for Baptist Churches Practicing Theology*, ed. Amy L. Chilton and Steven R. Harmon (Macon, GA: Mercer University Press, 2020), 26.

society as a whole. I have become so embarrassed by that failure that I could not reissue this volume without making a note of it and without exchanging the exclusive language of the 1970 edition to inclusive language. I know that this is hardly enough to rectify my failure, because sexism cannot be eliminated (anymore than racism) simply by changing words. But it is an important symbol of what we must do, because our language is a reflection of the reality we create. Sexism dehumanizes and kills, and it must be fought on every front.[3]

It is instructive that as a Black male Cone admits his own complicity in the marginalization and invisibility of Black women and reaches out to Black men not only in the academy but also in the Black church to become aware of the toxicity of sexism in the Black church. For several years Cone argued against the dangers of racism and its legacy of inferiority and subordination among people of color. Now he couples racism with sexism and hopes his students both in church and academy will take heed: "Any black male theologian or preacher who ignores sexism as a central problem in our society and church (as important as racism, because they are interconnected), is just as guilty of distorting the gospel as is a white theologian who does the same with racism. If we black male theologians do not take seriously the need to incorporate into our theology a critique of our sexist practices in the black community, then we have no right to complain when white theologians snub black theology."[4]

Cone not only called on Black men not to ignore the cry of Black women that they were marginalized and rendered invisible by Black men in church and family, but he also sought to create liberative space for Black women in Black theology. But there was an obstacle that Cone did not anticipate— Black men did Black theology out of the context of the Black male experience and universalized this experience and therefore spoke for Black women. Black women, as they highlighted their experience, identified the womanist

3. James H. Cone, *A Black Theology of Liberation*, fortieth anniversary ed. (Maryknoll, NY: Orbis Books, 2010), xx.
4. Cone, *A Black Theology of Liberation*, xx.

experience of struggle as the source of women's experience, from which they acted and reflected on the world of struggle and suffering.

I will examine the womanist perspectives of three thinkers who reference Black theology but also move beyond it, in part due to the hegemony of patriarchy, which renders theology and Christology incapable of offering liberation and salvation to all of God's children, especially Black women. We will look at the theological perspectives of Kelly Brown Douglas, Jacquelyn Grant, and Katie Cannon.

## Kelly Brown Douglas

Kelly Brown Douglas began theological studies as a student of James Cone with a central question: Is the God of Jesus Christ for or against Black liberation? With Cone's *A Black Theology of Liberation* as resource, she became convinced that God was on the side of the oppressed and that in a racist society such as the United States of America confidence in such a God empowered her in the struggle against racism. Her journey toward womanist theology began with Black theology's struggle and engagement with racism and the ensuing understanding that in her contextual situation, God and Christ were Black. "The image of a Black God gave me a new sense of pride in my own Blackness. . . . But as I developed an awareness of what it meant to be a woman in a sexist society I saw the limitations of the Black God and the Black Christ."[5] Douglas indicated that if Black theology helped her affirm pride of identity as a Black woman, it did not go far enough, as she had not yet dealt with the other equally important pole of her identity, her womanhood. She felt a sense of urgency in helping Black women in the community understand that sexism and patriarchy should not be relegated to the experience of the White woman but should also be dealt with by the Black woman. Sexism and patriarchy were sinful realities in the Black church

5. Kelly Brown Douglas, "Womanist Theology: What Is Its Relationship to Black Theology?" in *Black Theology: A Documentary History, 1980–1992*, ed. Gayraud Wilmore and James Cone (Maryknoll, NY: Orbis Books, 1992), 291.

and Black community. If the entire Black community were to be free, it had to set its sight on the eradication not only of racism but also of sexism. The harsh truth is, she left the door open to acknowledge the uni-dimensionality of Black theology. If Black theology helped her with the race question, she now had to confront the woman question. Granted the indispensable role of Black theology in addressing racism and White supremacy in American society, Douglas affirmed that it nonetheless did not affirm the Black woman experience. "Shaped by the Black power/civil rights movement out of which it emerged, Black theology focused only on one dimension of Black oppression—White racism. Its failure to utilize black women's experience further prevented it from developing an adequate analysis of black oppression. It did not address the multiple social burdens, that is, racism, sexism, classism, and heterosexism, which beset Black men and women. Consequently, it presented an image of God and Christ that was important in the fight for Black freedom. A Black God could not empower Black women as they confronted sexism."[6]

It is precisely at this point that Kelly Brown Douglas turns to Black faith and Black life for an answer to her earlier question, Is the God of Jesus Christ for or against Black liberation?

In a chapter entitled "A Father's Faith," Douglas calls attention to Tracy Martin, the father of Trayvon Martin, who, reflecting on the loss of his son at the hands of a cruel white world, said, "My heart is broken but my faith is unshattered." If on the one hand the faith of a father pointed to an exodus God who companions God's people on a journey in search of new life, on the other hand there is the faith of a nation that journeys with God through the wilderness and brings unexpected death to many others. "The faith of a nation gives way to a culture that negates Black life. The faith of a father affirms Black life in the midst of a culture of death."[7] It is something of a paradox that Black faith took root in the same soil that enslaved Black bodies, and this planting of faith was done in the name of God.

6. Douglas, "Womanist Theology," 291.

7. Kelly Brown Douglas, *Stand Your Ground: Black Bodies and the Justice of God* (Maryknoll, NY: Orbis Books, 2015), 137.

Douglas proffers a relationship not between faith and reason as we tend to do in a class in theology but between Black faith and Black life. She suggests that Black faith has to deal with the absurdities of life as it witnesses to a God who invites oppressed Black persons to relationship and friendship. In this sense faith becomes a response to join God in God's work of liberation: "Faith is a response to God. Faith is possible only if God acted and has initiated a relationship with human beings. Faith is the human response to God's invitation to be in relationship. Black faith represents a resounding yes to God's offer. This yes signals black people's belief in the power of God to right what is wrong in the world, even though they find themselves in the midst of a harsh absurdity of black life in Anglo-Saxon America."[8]

This faith in the divine relationship affirmed Black faith's confidence that the oppressed were made for freedom. "When Israel was in Egypt's land, Let my people go; Oppressed so hard they could not stand, Let my people go; Go down, Moses, 'way down in Egypt land; Tell ole Pharoah, Let my people go."[9] Black faith as enshrined in the spirituals affirmed that Black bodies were not created by God to be bought and sold but were created to draw on and from the freedom of God. God made them and meant them for freedom. Songs of freedom provided liberative space for plotting and planning a new future outside of the hearing and suspicion of the enslaver. While Black faith acknowledged the pain in Black communities inflicted on Black bodies, through the song Blacks did more than acknowledge pain; they planned for the transformation of self and community. The spirituals became a strategy for liberation and transformation. Douglas points out that through the song Black faith seeks not only to change the perspective of victims but also to use Black history and Black culture to dismantle oppression and point to the dignity and worth of Black life. "It is well established that music has been essential to Black people as they have navigated a society that has seen them as chattel. Whether it is spirituals or the blues, music has provided a way for Black people to communicate about the contradictions

---

8. Douglas, *Stand Your Ground*, 139.

9. James H. Cone, *The Spirituals and the Blues* (New York: Seabury, 1972), 44.

and hardships as well as the joys and triumphs of black living."[10] Black faith would also proclaim:

> Don't be weary, traveller
> Come along home to Jesus
> My head get wet with the midnight dew
> Come along home to Jesus
> Angels bear me witness too
> Come along home to Jesus.[11]

According to Douglas, the invitation to come home to Jesus was not an eschatological hope but a call to "free space" for Black bodies to live into their reality of being made in God's image. When God calls a Black body home, that call is to live in the fullness of a body created in the image of God. "Recognizing home as the place to which God calls black bodies makes even more poignant Sybrina Fulton's observation that her son, Travon was simply trying to get home. According to the black faith tradition this means that Travon was simply trying to get to that space where he could be free—that is, to be the Travon God created him to be."[12]

At the center of Black faith is the cross of Christ:

> Dey crucified my Lord
> An' He never said a mumblin' word
> De crucified my Lord
> An' He never said a mumblin' word
> Not a word, not a word, not a word.[13]

At the cross Christ empties himself of all power and privilege and enters into solidarity with the crucified bodies. "It is no wonder then that the Christ hymn in Philippians (2:5–11) is a text often recited in various black

10. Douglas, Stand Your Ground, 141.
11. Douglas, *Stand Your Ground*, 153.
12. Douglas, *Stand Your Ground*, 153–54.
13. Douglas, *Stand Your Ground*, 177.

churches. . . . 'He humbled himself, and became obedient unto death, even unto the cross.'"

Again, Black faith would chant:

> Oh when I come to die
> Give me Jesus
> Give me Jesus
> You may have the world
> Give me Jesus.[14]

It was clear for the community of Black faith that Jesus would go all the way, even through the valley of deepest darkness. God's freedom as expressed in God's love for victims knows no limits.

Black faith understood that Jesus was present as savior, friend, and hope. The one who was their hope and liberator also suffered with them at the hands of an unjust oppressor. Their helper was a friend in times of trouble. The prayer of an enslaved woman illustrates a connection between Black faith and Black life.

> Dear Massa Jesus, we all uns beg Ooner [you] come make us a call dis yere day. We is nutting but poor Ethiopian women and people ain't tink much 'bout we. We ain't trust any of dem great high people for come to we Church, but do' you is de one great Massa, great too much dan massa Linkum, you ain't shame to care for we African people.
>
> Come to me, dear Massa Jesus. De sun, he too hot too much, de road am dat long and boggy sandy and we ain't got no buggy for send and fetch Ooner [you]. But Massa, you member how you walked the hard walk up Calvary and ain't weary but tink about we all de way. We know you ain't weary for to come to we.[15]

14. Douglas, *Stand Your Ground*, 178.
15. Harold Carter, *The Prayer Tradition of Black People* (Valley Forge, PA: Judson, 1976), 29.

An African woman sums up her prayer to Jesus: "You ain't shame to care for we African people." Deuteronomy 7:21: "Have no dread of them, for the Lord your God, who is present with you, is a great and awesome God."

In the end, Douglas warns that Christians cannot afford to forget the cross; neither should they glorify the cross. She fears that glorifying the cross could be understood as glorifying suffering. Douglas agrees with Delores Williams that in the end meaning should be found for the Christian not in the suffering engendered by the cross but in the triumph of the resurrection of Christ. "There is no doubt that an emphasis on Jesus' crucifixion has perpetuated human suffering. . . . It has also unquestionably led to the unnecessary acceptance of suffering. [Williams] is right to assert that there is 'no power in the blood' of one who is victimized by crucifying realities. However, this is not what the crucifixion-resurrection event suggests. And it certainly has not been the prevailing meaning of the cross within the black faith tradition, even though it is the cross that has provided black people with a full understanding of the presence of God in their lives."[16]

Douglas insists that Black faith must maintain a robust connection between the cross and the "empty tomb," as Black faith seeks to give content to the meaning of the resurrection of Christ. The cross anchors the resurrection in history. "It makes clear that the evil that God overcomes is historical. . . . Understanding the resurrection in the light of the cross prevents the resurrection from becoming the otherworldly triumph over cosmic evil. . . . It is the connection between the cross and resurrection that has enabled black people to know that God, as revealed in Jesus, intimately understands their suffering and pain."[17] It is clear that for Douglas cross and resurrection are interlinked. The cross of Christ anchors the resurrection in history, and God takes on the principalities and powers that assail Black faith. It is through the power of the resurrection that a community informed by Black faith is able to exit traditions that demean and stultify the humanity

16. Douglas, *Stand Your Ground*, 187.
17. Douglas, *Stand Your Ground*, 187.

of God's children. It is through cross and resurrection that a community of oppressed persons can witness to an exodus from victimization and exploitation through the power of the resurrection. The resurrection of Jesus points to God's commitment to overcome the principalities and powers that frustrate God's plan for the "crucified class." "To restore to life those whose bodies are the particular targets of the world's violence is to signal the triumph over crucifying violence and death itself. . . . The meaning of one's life . . . is not found in death."[18]

For Douglas, cross and resurrection are interlinked because the cross of Christ points to the specificity and historicity of the event of the gospel of Christ taking on significance in the social and contextual situation in which "crucified peoples" find themselves. Black faith and praxis are conjoined as Black faith means leaving Egypt, as oppressed persons relate faith to the concrete conditions that affect both body and soul. Interestingly, for Douglas God's activity in history in a particular time and place has significance, as Christ died and rose from the dead for all who suffer and hunger for the justice and freedom from the one who forgave sinners and entered into solidarity with the poor. The coming of Jesus and his ministry among the poor provide the point of departure for the new life that Christ offers through his life, death, and resurrection. For Douglas, womanist Christology announces the scandal of the cross: "the preferential option for the poor," that God through Jesus sides with the poor, and in the end, that was what got him killed. It was not his death that was redemptive but his life in its entirety that was devoted to God and fellowship with women and many sinners outside the mainstream of society. The cross then became a signal and sign of God's gift of life made possible through the transformative power of the resurrection. Black faith highlights the cross and resurrection as interpretive keys that make central the life of Jesus with the poor and despised, reminding them that God has entered into solidarity with the least of these, making their condition his own.

18. Douglas, *Stand Your Ground*, 188.

## Jacquelyn Grant

In a poignant essay, "Womanist Jesus and the Mutual Struggle for Liberation," Jacquelyn Grant points out that the existence of Black women could
be characterized by the term "trouble," and, although women such as Harriet
Tubman could point to the power and presence of Jesus, this happened in the
midst of trouble. "She had reached the 'state' which she had perceived to be
like heaven—freedom—the long awaited reality."[19] Tubman became aware
that trouble was ubiquitous, and yet Jesus was "a present hope in times of
trouble." The dilemma that contemporary Black women face is that Jesus as
presented by the church is imprisoned by patriarchy, White supremacy, and
the privileged class, argues Grant.

The church as institution often allows men to define who Jesus is in relation to women. Grant comments that one of the central questions that Jesus
addresses to the church is, "Who do you say that I am?" This question, Grant
argues, is also addressed to women, but men seek to answer for women. One
problem here is that in men answering for women, Jesus is imprisoned by
the privileged class within the prison of patriarchy. "An aspect of the social
context in which Christianity as we know it developed, and in which we now
live, is 'patriarchy.' Defined in the male consciousness, patriarchy assumes
male dominance and control, making normative the centrality of men and
the marginality of women" (131). Maleness becomes idolatrous as men lord it
over women and stand in for God. Another problem is that it becomes difficult for Christians to think of Jesus outside of maleness. Thus, Jesus becomes
imprisoned by patriarchy's elevation of maleness as the essence of Christology. The obsession with maleness as a conceptual tool for understanding
Jesus distorts the personhood of Jesus Christ. The way forward for women,
according to Grant, is to liberate Jesus from the prison of maleness and allow
women's experience to become one of the sources for understanding the per-

19. Jacquelyn Grant, "Womanist Jesus and the Mutual Struggle for Liberation," in *The
Recovery of Black Presence: An Interdisciplinary Exploration*, ed. Randall C. Bailey and Jacquelyn Grant (Nashville: Abingdon, 1995), 129. Hereafter, page references from this work
will be given in parentheses in the text.

son and mission of Jesus. Seeing Jesus through the eyes of women empowers women to speak of Jesus from the vantage point of their own experience and to see themselves in the biblical narrative. "Seeing reality through the eyes of women has led to the rereading of biblical texts and the revisiting of biblical and theological interpretations. . . . The fact that the presence of women in the Bible was important, and that Jesus was not only not anti-woman, but in fact was always affirming of women" (132). The historical imprisonment of Jesus by notions of the maleness of Jesus as central to his identity and his relationship with women must be abolished and destroyed. Women must be empowered to answer Jesus's question "Who do you say that I am?" from the perspective of their own experience. The problem of sexism is highlighted as women push back against a negative Christology in which their humanity and personhood are demeaned and diminished through the practice and teaching of the church.

And yet Grant acknowledges that the sin of racism is more pervasive that the sin of sexism. Grant puts it this way: "For African American women, however, the question is much broader than the sin of sexism. Racism, in the view of many, has been the basic defining character in the lives of African American women in North America. . . . Unfortunately, the church has not escaped this sinful reality. On the contrary, the church has been the bastion of the sin of racism. This is reflected not only in the practice of much of its populace, but in the structures and in the theologies of the churches" (133).

According to Grant, when Christians fail to challenge an understanding of Christ that promotes the evils of racism, then Christology becomes a tool of White racist ideology. One way in which this ideology is expressed unwittingly is for White feminists to universalize their experience and seek to speak on behalf of all women. Grant points out that what in fact happens is that a White feminist perspective is highlighted. White women are encouraged by Grant to identify the particularity of their privileged position and acknowledge that they present and represent a White feminism. It is in this context that Black women are allowed to identify their own needs and to express from their own perspective who Jesus Christ is for them.

"In the White church tradition, Jesus has functioned as a status quo figure. Because, historically speaking, Christology was constructed in the context of White supremacy ideology and domination, Christ has functioned to legitimate these social and political realities. Essentially, Christ has been White" (135).

Grant references the work of James Cone and Albert Cleage to support her claim that notions of a White Christ are predominant not only in White culture and society but also in the Black church and society. In the dominant American and European culture in which purity and beauty are signified by whiteness, it becomes understandable that a White Christ would be embraced by both Black church and culture. A consequence of this way of thinking and believing is the conclusion and affirmation that Black people are not created in the image of God. Grant is emphatic that the way forward for womanist ways of believing and understanding Black faith is that the White God-Christ must be eliminated from the Black-womanist experience and a Black-womanist Christ must emerge.

Elaine Brown Crawford, in *Hope in the Holler: A Womanist Theology*, supports Grant's highlighting of the scourge of racism and how racism is often disguised as servanthood. Crawford affirms Grant's claim that there is a sense in which Christians are called to serve in the tradition of Jesus, yet the reality on the ground points up the expectation that Black women are "the servants of servants." Like Jesus, Black women are crucified, and their crucifixion has "included having their families broken up when children were separated from parents, rapes, brutality, and the physical exploitation that Black women have been forced to endure."[20] Crawford reminds us that Grant refers to the expected subordination of Black women in the work culture as the "sin of servanthood." Non-White people were believed to be the servant class who were created for the express purpose of providing service for White people. The bottom line here is that Black women were treated as property, seen as inferior and meant for servanthood.

---

20. Elaine Brown Crawford, *Hope in the Holler: A Womanist Theology* (Louisville: Westminster John Knox, 2002), 92.

Grant puts her finger on the complexity and mystery of what it means to be human. In the church we often understand human beings as creatures created by God, created for relationships with God, persons, and the created world. And yet the proclivity to exploit those who are weak, and oppressed by race, class, and gender, points to the propensity of human beings to be in bondage to sin. Persons who are economically poor are treated as property.

According to Professor Grant, the way forward is the acknowledgment and embrace of a womanist Jesus. There is a mutual struggle for liberation, according to Grant. Grant points out that an examination of the experience of Black women indicates that there is a mutual interdependence of the need of Black women for Jesus and Jesus for Black. "The Jesus of African American women has suffered a triple bondage or imprisonment as well. Jesus has been held captive to the sin of patriarchy (sexism), the sin of White supremacy (racism) and the sin of privilege ( classism). As such Jesus has been used to keep women in their 'proper place'; to keep Blacks meek, mild, and docile in the face of the brutal forms of dehumanization; and to ensure the servility of servants."[21] Grant concludes that both Jesus and African American women are in need of liberation from sexism, racism, and classism. The words of Jesus need to be set free in the church, as a point of departure, so that both women and Jesus may be liberated. In spite of the imprisonment of Jesus and women in the church, Jesus has remained central in African American women's life and faith. Jesus is experienced in their communities quite differently from what was intended by their oppressors. Grant highlights five centers from which African American women gain an identity and strength in relation to Jesus.

1. *Jesus as cosufferer.* A central theme in womanist Christology, according to Grant, is that the divine suffers with the oppressed—highlighting the divine humility. It is this notion of cosuffering with Christ that provides a center from which African women draw their strength. They learned to walk with Jesus and, through Jesus, share in divine suffering.

21. Grant, "Womanist Jesus," 138.

2. *Jesus as equalizer*. In the Black church, African American women and men embraced notions of being made in the image of God—and this sense of the *imago Dei* was pivotal in their sense of belonging to a human covenant with God in which all people, by virtue of being in covenant with God, share in God's covenant with the human family. The cross of Christ points to the event and the place where divine salvation is offered to all—not just to men, White and Black, but also to Black women. Because of this, Jesus came and died not only for Whites but for all, including Black women. It is in this sense that Jesus is the equalizer, as Jesus is for all, as Jesus removes all limitations.

3. *Jesus as freedom*. However, a goal of the Christian life is not equality with others, as this could lead to the temptation to become like other people—especially in a culture where things are worshiped. If one aspires to equality in the context of the covenant with the people of God, this must lead to freedom with the conviction that "for freedom Christ has set us free" (Gal. 5:1). Grant sums up her emphasis on freedom: "'Equal to whom?' Do we merely seek to be equal to those who practice oppression against others? Is the goal simply that we not be among the oppressed? Freedom is the central message of Jesus Christ and the gospel, and is concisely summarized in Luke 4:18."[22] The experience of African American women teaches that those who are followers of Jesus are children of freedom.

4. *Jesus as sustainer*. Grant reminds us that in the experience of African American women—Sojourner Truth, Fannie Lou Hamer, and Jarena Lee, for example—the journey toward freedom becomes tedious and difficult. In this context much depends on the power of Christ's presence, as Jesus is experienced as the sustainer. On the journey toward freedom, Black people remind us in lyrical prose that "Jesus is a shelter in a time of storm, a doctor in the sick room, a lawyer in the court house, and one who makes a way out of no way."[23] Often in contexts where the family is dysfunctional or absent, Jesus is called on as a father to the fatherless, or as a mother to the motherless, and as a friend to the friendless. It is this confidence in the power of

22. Grant, "Womanist Jesus," 140.
23. Grant, "Womanist Jesus," 140.

the presence of Jesus that sustains black faith in the journey toward dignity and liberation.

5. *Jesus as liberator.* The central challenge facing womanist theologians according to Grant is to acknowledge the minimal baseline of engaging a tridimensional analysis of oppression—racism, sexism, and classism. This takes on the notion of a male God and insists that theological language that excludes people of color must move into multidimensional analysis. It is the notion of Jesus as liberator that "empowers Black women to continue the womanist tradition of liberating Jesus and themselves."[24]

### Katie Cannon

Katie Cannon, in her essay "Transformative Grace," points out that as a girl growing up in the Presbyterian church, she surmised that grace had to be more than a word recited in the liturgy. If grace were to become incarnate in community and in the existential situation, then the word had to become enfleshed in order for transformation to become a reality in community and in the social situation in which she along with others celebrated God's redeeming work manifest in Christ Jesus and the struggle for liberation. It was clear that for Cannon there were two sides to grace—God's disclosure of forgiveness and mercy manifest in the life, death, and resurrection of Jesus Christ, and the participation of the community of the oppressed in acts of liberation. Cannon highlights a starting point: "As a black Presbyterian, grace was the basic motif of our lives. I have long known that grace is an unmerited gift from God. However, not until recently did I understand grace as sacred, life transforming power for those whose identities are shaped by multiple forces at odds with the dominant culture, primarily those of race, sex and class. God's freely given gift of grace enables us to resist the forces of death and degradation arrayed against us and to affirm our dignity as beloved persons created in the image of God."[25]

24. Grant, "Womanist Jesus," 140.
25. Katie Geneva Cannon, "Transformative Grace," in *Feminist and Womanist Essays in*

For Cannon, talk about grace includes talk about sin. Grace is God's gift that allows oppressed persons to overcome situations of death and alienation from God, the source of life, and from God's creation. Because grace is freely given, Cannon is clear that grace is not merely a response to sins of race, sex, and class but God's presence is freely experienced among God's people. Through grace God restores God's relationship with God's creation and with us.

The central idea that Cannon seeks to highlight in her essay is how may womanist theologians and those who embrace the Christian faith as a lifestyle translate grace—the activity of God on behalf of those who suffer and are heavy-laden—into practice. How may the children of God give more than lip service to God's presence of justifying and liberating grace? Cannon puts it this way:

> Each and every morning I stood tall, crossed my heart, and pledged allegiance to the flag of the United States of America. I recited the Lord's Prayer, quoted the Beatitudes, and answered questions from the Missouri Synod Lutheran catechism. Yet at the same time I lived in a world that demanded and commanded that I go to the back of the bus even though I paid the same fare. Before the age of five, the unbending social codes of conduct between blacks and whites required that I go through back doors and drink out of "colored" water fountains. This racial etiquette was traumatic, and it was violent. So complete was the circle of segregationist laws, the rigidly enforced codes of white supremacy, that it was against the law for me to play in tax-supported public schools.[26]

It is clear that the practice of worship in church and pedagogy at school was seared into the consciousness of Katie Cannon as she struggled against notions of invisibility and exclusion for not being allowed as a five-year-old to play with her peers in the public park. According to Katie, what was at

---

*Reformed Dogmatics*, ed. Amy Plantinga Pauw and Serene Jones (Louisville: Westminster John Knox, 2006), 139.

26. Cannon, "Transformative Grace," 141.

stake was the degradation of Black bodies and notions that she was inferior to White people. Cannon forces us to ask for the meaning of grace when a child is set aside because of notions of an ugly body and an underdeveloped intellect and seen as belonging to a culture that is underdeveloped. What does it mean to recite the Lord's Prayer in this context? It is clear that grace means more than mouthing liturgies and sharing in long prayers. The challenge is how to embrace grace as an expression of liberation when the goal of liberation conjoined with grace is the transformation of a situation—even a situation of faith in which the body is demeaned as Black children and women are excluded because they are perceived as ugly and not embraced as recipients of saving grace. For Katie Cannon, who was the first Black woman to be ordained in the Presbyterian Church in America, the gospel of Christ addressed the personal as well as the social context in which people engage in the quest for racial and economic justice. The theologian must work within the struggle to relate the Christian faith to the concrete conditions that affect both body and soul. According to Cannon, grace must become more than a word that is translated and interpreted—grace must become incarnational as the ecclesial community embodies the life and ministry of Jesus.

In no uncertain way, Cannon reminds us that as grace is enfleshed and becomes more than an idea, new ways of thinking and acting must be conjoined. "First and foremost, grace is a divine gift of redeeming love that empowers African Americans to confront shocking, absurd, death-dealing disjunctions in life, so that when we look at our outer struggles and inner strength we see interpretive possibilities for creative change. Second, grace is the indwelling of God's spirit that enables Christians of African descent to live conscious lives of thanksgiving, by deepening our knowledge of forgiveness given in Christ."[27] What is advocated here by Cannon is the uniting of theory and practice, of word and deed, of knowing and doing. Those who know the will of Christ will do the will of Christ. It is not enough to interpret an idea; the idea must become enfleshed. The good news according to

27. Cannon, "Transformative Grace," 143–44.

Cannon is that the oppressive situation does not have the last word. The oppressive situation that demeans and diminishes God's children is challenged by the practice of liberation rooted in the empirical situation as African Americans name the evil and sin embedded in the existential situation as they work for and pray for the in-breaking of a new humanity. Grace means identifying with those who are homeless, hungry, and told they have ugly bodies and discovering that they have assumed the identity and form of the crucified Christ.

According to Cannon, grace is the indwelling of God's spirit that enables Christians of African descent to live lives of thanksgiving. Thanksgiving becomes a way of life because the Spirit mediates the presence of Christ among us. Paul sums up the activity of the spirit of freedom—"Now the Lord is the Spirit, and where the Spirit of the Lord is, there is freedom. And all of us, with unveiled faces, seeing the glory of the Lord as though reflected in a mirror, are being transformed into the same image from one degree of glory to another; for this comes from the Lord, the Spirit" (2 Cor. 3:17–18).

With the gift of grace the Spirit of God creates spaces for dialogue in which the oppressed name evil and demeaning practices that allow many of God's children to question their humanity. Through the gift of grace engendered by the Spirit of God, the body of people of African descent becomes a site of liberation and thanksgiving. Grace means that people of African descent are free to accept themselves with the confidence that they are accepted by God. When the church or classroom becomes Black sacred space, all bodies are welcomed. This I believe has been one of the gifts of Black churches over the years—providing Black sacred space to which all persons are welcomed and invited to accept themselves as daughters and sons of God. In this Black sacred space called the church of Christ, weary travelers find rest, and many who were alienated discover in Christ, through the Spirit, a healing presence as God's love is poured into our hearts. Black faith as the praxis of Jesus liberates us from dependence on the ruling class and structures and systems that are oppressive. Grace transposes a life of despair and loss of meaning to one of transformation and empowerment.

# Black Theology after James Cone

The impetus to write on Black theology after James Cone raises the need to talk about Cone's contribution to Black theology. While it is often mentioned that Cone was the father of Black theology, Cone was not the founder or originator of Black theology, as scholars such as Howard Thurman, W. E. B. Du Bois, Benjamin Mays, and Mary McCloud Bethune preceded Cone's articulation of the Black experience as a primary source and resource for Black theology. However, something new happened in Cone's elaboration of Black theology, and one index of the new that emerged in his talk about the "Word of God as the praxis of Jesus" was his insistence that the reality of the oppressed and oppressors must always be the context for the articulation of theology. Cone quite early made a connection between his theological project in the context of the Black experience in the United States and what was happening in the Third World. Cone, himself a child of the Black church, understood that the renewal of Black life in the United States was integrally linked to the Black church reality. Here we look at Cone's attempt to critically evaluate his iteration of Black theology by looking beyond the Black experience as it was understood in the US context as he turned to the Third World and placed his work in conversation with sisters and brothers outside the US context. It is fair to suggest that Cone often tested his approach to Black theology with conversations with Karl Barth, Paul Tillich, and Reinhold Niebuhr. The conversation with sisters and brothers outside the United States frequently pushed him to deal with another context in which racism was not the primary theological problem. In this context, Cone had to reach for a way to talk about colonialism, classism, and poverty as central theological problems. Here he made theological space for conversations and articulations of theology and ethics as questions of violence and structural oppression took center stage. However, Cone never strayed far from the centrality of the Black church. I would wager that even when in his first book he seemed to have deviated from the Black church in his romance with Malcolm X and Stokely Carmichael, he was in search of new ways to talk about issues of power in the context of the gospel of Christ.

Cone anchored his work in the Black church, and this provided ontological status for his articulation of Black existence.

There will be three main themes in this chapter. The first is what Cone calls "Black theology and the Third World." What would the new future for Black theology and the Black diaspora look like from the vantage point of a theology of the Black experience. Would liberation for African Americans also include peoples in the African diaspora? Would their futures be conjoined? Would liberation of African Americans include Africa and the African diaspora?

The second emphasis is Cone's view of the church in which the Christ of the church becomes the point of departure for talk about theology. We will investigate how Cone talks about salvation and liberation in inclusive ways that would apply to Black folks in the United States and outside the United States who do not ascribe to the Christian approach to salvation that is grounded in the church's understanding of Jesus as the Christ.

Finally, what does transformation engendered by a commitment to the gospel of Christ look like in the context of Black theology?

## Black Theology and the Third World

I had the wonderful experience of being in the first cohort of graduate students in the PhD program at Union Theological Seminary under the direction of Professor James Cone. I recall vividly in the second class period, as he paced the floor and articulated in passionate language his conviction of the Black American experience providing a context for his articulation of Black theology. I raised my hand to ask my first question. "Professor Cone," I inquired. "What does Black theology have to do with Jamaica?" Cone's answer was equally passionate. "Nothing," he said. I came to believe that he lived with my question, as in subsequent years he broached the question of Black theology and the Third World. Cone paid his first visit to Jamaica in 1979 and presented a paper to the United Theological Colleges of the West

Indies, "What Is Christian Theology?" The president of the college in an editorial spoke of Cone's visit as initiating a time of transition and theological exploration in the Caribbean.

> It marks the end of the dominance of Western patterns of thought and methods of formulation as well as the flowering of new and creative insights which, for the most part, come out of the Third World and are influenced by exposure of sensitive Christians to the wretchedness of the earth. It is becoming possible to speak responsibly of God out of the concrete historical situations and experiences of ordinary people, devoid of abstractions, abstruse language and speculative methods. It is becoming possible to understand and interpret God's nature, activity and purpose by reflecting on those situations of oppressions, deprivation, and degradation which are the common lot of the majority of humankind and also on their struggles and aspirations for that human dignity to which they are entitled.[1]

Cone's lecture was included as the main article in the journal edited by President Watty, with a response by Jamaican theologian Dr. Burchell Taylor. Since this was such an important time of transition and exploration by Caribbean churches and theologians, I will highlight Cone's attempt to relate Black theology to Jamaica and Taylor's response.

Cone's point of departure in addressing the topic "What is Christian theology?" was the broad strokes of the divine activity in the world on behalf of oppressed persons, and he conjoined this talk about the divine in the world with an appeal to Scripture. Cone's primary source was Scripture and its appeal to God as liberator of the oppressed.

> My contention that the scripture is the story of God's liberation of the poor also applies to the New Testament, where the story is carried to universal

---

1. William W. Watty, editorial, *Caribbean Journal of Religious Studies* 3, no. 2 (September 1980): iii–iv.

dimensions.... The meaning of Jesus Christ is found in God's will to make liberation not simply the property of one people but of all humankind. God became a poor Jew and thus identified with the helpless in Israel. The Cross of Jesus is nothing but God's will to be with and like the poor. The Resurrection means that God achieved victory over oppression, so that the poor no longer have to be determined by their poverty.[2]

Cone insisted that the pivot to Scripture was his way of highlighting Scripture as the primary source for doing theology. Cone was not yet discovering the word of God in the community of the oppressed or in the existential situation in which people struggle with various forms of oppression. The closest Cone came to speak of divine revelation in the community of the oppressed in this lecture was to suggest that authentic theology should reflect "the rhythm and mood, the passion and ecstasy, the joy and sorrow of a people in struggle to free themselves from the shackles of oppression. This theology must be black because the people are black."[3]

Cone most likely lost his audience in his proposal that theology should become Black. Jamaica in particular, and the Caribbean in general, has never been at peace with blackness. Both Marcus Garvey and the Rastafari faith were shunned by people from the Caribbean with notions that Caribbean people should see God through their own spectacles or that God may be associated with a Black man in Ethiopia called Haile Selassie. Theologian Taylor refused to make any connection with the address given by Cone and seems to suggest that Jamaicans need to do their own thing as they seek to be contextual. Taylor puts it this way: "The use of the qualifying term 'Caribbean' indicates that a Caribbean theology will be overtly and self-consciously contextual. It will be a theology arising out of the Caribbean for the Caribbean. This means that first and foremost the theology will be related to its context with the direct aim and purpose of speaking meaningfully to the people within the context, dealing with issues that are directly related

2. James H. Cone, "What Is Christian Theology?" *Caribbean Journal of Religious Studies* 3, no. 2 (September 1980): 1–12.

3. Cone, "What Is Christian Theology?," 9.

to its context, dealing with the issues that are directly related to the people's life and experience."[4]

In his important book *For My People: Black Theology and the Black Church*, Cone acknowledged that in the development of Black theology from the American perspective, European theology served as a model for him and others who sought to relate Black theology to the Black church and Black religion. The catalyst that made them rethink European theology as source and resource for Black theology was the Caribbean thinker Frantz Fanon. "Although Frantz Fanon's *The Wretched of the Earth* was the catalyst that drew our attention away from Europe, it was Gayraud Wilmore and Charles Long who accepted the radical implications of his challenge and pushed us toward Africa as the critical source for the development of a black theology based on black religion."[5]

In a chapter in which Cone related Black theology to the Third World, he indicated that Wilmore articulated the shift that was imperative theologically if Black theology would affirm its African roots and enter into solidarity with countries in the Third World. Wilmore articulated the need for a radical shift if Black faith would move away from the culture of White domination that shaped Christian faith. This shift of Black faith would announce the radical solidarity with God among the oppressed of every race and nation, as the suffering of oppressed people was understood as God's suffering. Wilmore frames the issue:

> The violence perpetuated upon the oppressed is violence against God. Their death is God's assassination. But God raised Jesus from death and because we see in him the faces of the poor, oppressed peoples of the world . . . black theologians speak unabashedly of the black Messiah, this oppressed and assassinated God who is risen to give life and hope to all who are oppressed. This black Messiah who is the oppressed man of God,

4. Burchell K. Taylor, "Caribbean Theology," *Caribbean Journal of Religious Studies* 3, no. 2 (September 1980): 17–18.

5. James H. Cone, *For My People: Black Theology and the Black Church* (Maryknoll, NY: Orbis Books, 1984), 72.

who is seen in the faces of the Black poor, oppressed black people, and whose death and resurrection is their rising to new life and power, is the meaning of the gospel of liberation that stands opposite to the ideology of domination by which the God of the Christian culture of Europe and America was fabricated before and after the Enlightenment.[6]

In an essay, "Black Theology and Third World Theologies," Cone begins to join a conversation with Third World theologies as he points out the thirst and interest in the Third World for liberation in political and socioeconomic terms. The gospel of Christ was introduced to many of these countries by the missionary community. Cone was insistent that oppressed peoples in these countries were impacted by European and North American missionaries who effected a divorce between salvation and liberation as salvation was presented as a spiritual force bereft of acknowledgment of the whole person. Something of a breakthrough occurred in the Third World as communities of the oppressed in their encounter with the Bible discovered that the Bible concerned the whole person, including the physical well-being of persons. "The neglect of the political and economic aspects of the gospel by European and North American missionaries came to be understood as a deliberate cover-up by oppressors so the Third World victims would not challenge the unjust international order. As long as Third World peoples believe that the meaning of the gospel is defined by Europe and North America, they could not develop theological perspectives that would challenge their domination by the First World."[7] It was of first importance that Third World theologies begin to develop a theological principle that would help them question colonialism and different forms of oppression in a theological way. Cone was correct in pointing out that for many Third World countries the press for political liberation was the catalyst that engendered rebellion against colonial rule. He sums up the

6. Cited by Cone, *For My People*, 140.

7. James Cone, " Black Theology and Third World Theologies," *Chicago Theological Seminary Register* 62, no. 1 (Winter 1983): 3. Hereafter, page references from this work will be given in parentheses in the text.

way forward in several Third World countries, as victims of imperialism and colonialism struggle to formulate their understanding of freedom. "The precise character of the liberation emphasized depended upon the political needs of the country as defined by people struggling to liberate themselves from foreign domination. Africans began to speak of a distinct African theology with a special interest in indigenization of the gospel so they would not have to become European in order to be Christians. Latin Americans spoke of theology with an exclusive emphasis on liberation" (3). In the Caribbean context, the dependence on colonial theology was fulsome and caused us to neglect the Caribbean context as our gaze was turned toward Europe. As Caribbean people engaged the God of Europe, there was a real danger God would become a foreigner and not able to address our needs in the homeland.

However, Cone began to see similarities between Third World theologies and Black theology. Both approaches to theology articulate the need to reread the Bible in light of the poor people's struggle toward freedom. This was important from the time of slavery in the New World, where oppressed enslaved people discovered that they could not trust the interpretation their masters and in many cases missionaries gave to the Scripture. As poor people read the Bible for themselves, they understood the "hermeneutical privilege" of the poor and the promise of the divine presence in times of trouble.

Cone highlights the aspirational key that the future of Black and Third World theologies proffer in their embrace of the Word of God as the praxis of Jesus. "This means that to do liberation theology, one must make a commitment, an option for the poor and against those who are responsible for their poverty. Because liberation theology is not simply something to be learned and taught in colleges and seminaries but to be created only in the struggles of the poor. . . . How can we participate in the liberation of the poor from oppression, if we do not know *who* the poor are and *why* they live in poverty?" (8).

Theologians of Black and Third World theologies are called on to engage in social, economic, and political analysis, as what is at stake is the questioning of the status quo and the exposure of who benefits from the exploitation of the poor. Indispensable tools are the investigation of the role of race, class, and gender in the sociological analysis that is required.

Cone suggests that there are two levels at which it is important to talk about differences between Black and Third World theologies—sociopolitical liberation and cultural liberation. "Black theologians have been adamant in their insistence that the God of the Bible is a political God who had identified divine righteousness with the bodily liberation of the poor. The differences between African and Black theologians on this point have led some African theologians, like John Mbiti, to say that African and Black theologies have nothing to do with each other. But the presence of Black theology in southern Africa had rendered Mbiti's statement problematic. For Desmond Tutu . . . says that Black and African theologies are soul mates and not antagonists" (9).

He highlights an essential distinction between Black and African theology. While it is true that Black theology seeks to relate the gospel of Jesus Christ to the political situation, this does not exclude the essential ingredient of spiritual liberation. What is of first importance according to Cone is not to reduce the gospel to notions of spirituality that do not take the plight and situation of the oppressed as the essential context for talk about liberation. "When the sufferings of the poor are individualized and privatized, it becomes difficult to identify their sufferings with God without challenging the existing socio-political arrangements responsible for their suffering" (9). There is a fear that suffering becomes intellectualized and unrelated to the existential plight of the poor.

This seems to be one of the problems between Black and Latin American theologies. While Black theology emphasizes race as a theological problem, Latin Americans ignore race in their highlighting of class analysis, which is understandable, since their methodology is influenced by Marxism. On the other hand, Black theologians would emphasize race, as they live in a racist society shaped by 250 years of slavery. Cone frames the conversation between Black and Latin American theologies. "Unfortunately Black theologians have not always been sensitive to class oppression or the role of U.S. imperialism in relation to the Third world. . . . Therefore Latin Americans have rightly asked about a social analysis in our theology that critiques capitalism. In this dialogue with Latin theologians, we have come to realize the importance of Marxism as a tool for social analysis" (10).

If on the one hand Latin American theologians have not embraced race analysis, Black theologians have been slow to acknowledge and embrace class analysis. Cone suggests that one way forward is to examine the way Black and Latin American theologians read the Bible and further examine the role of theologies in the struggle for liberation.

There is a sociological baseline in all these theologies of liberation. The common ground is that all communities that give rise to these theologies are affected and shaped by poverty and high rates of unemployment. Martin Luther King Jr., in commenting on the economic distance between the poverty in the Black ghettos of the United States and the wealth in the White enclaves, speaks of "an island of poverty in an ocean of wealth." And this is the case the world over, except in Third World nations, where the primary theological problem and sociological reality is not racism but classism. The implication for the theological task is that it is not enough to focus on either race or class; a method that is inclusive of both approaches must be identified. The way forward is the embrace of a praxiological method for theology that addresses the situations in both First World and Third World countries. The way forward is action on behalf of and with the oppressed that is informed by reflection. Cone acknowledges that this methodology emerged out of the Third World but was implicit in Black theology. "When the question is asked, 'How do we do theology?' black and Third World theologians agree that theology is not the first act but rather the second. Although our Latin American brothers and sisters . . . were the first to explicate this methodological point, it was already present and now reaffirmed in all our theologies. The first act is both a religio-cultural affirmation and a political commitment in behalf of the liberation of the poor and voiceless of our countries."[8] Perhaps Cone was correct in suggesting that this praxiological methodology that prioritizes the action-reflection methodology was implicit but not explicit in the method

8. Cone, *For My People*, 147.

that informs Black theology. In the Third World, the political and theological necessity is to allow the Word of God to break through in the praxis of Jesus as written in Matthew 25:35–36: "I was hungry and you gave me food, I was thirsty and you gave me something to drink, . . . I was naked and you gave me clothing, . . . I was in prison you visited me." In much of the Third World, this Word of God that confronts us in the life and deeds of Jesus engages us not merely as an ethical injunction but as a mandate of the gospel of Christ. In much of the Third World, theology begins with the practice of liberation for the oppressed. The initial impulse to do theology in this setting is to be there for the oppressed with acts of kindness.

This methodology that prioritizes the action-reflection way of life goes a little further than Cone's call for solidarity with the least of these. Cone lamented that African Americans tend to treat oppressed persons from Third World countries the way White people treat them. This points to one of the limits of Black theology in the way it is structured and focused on an understanding of the Black experience. Often he speaks of the Black experience as the Black church experience or as the cultural experience of Black people in America, and Black theology seeks to ground its way of talking about God and outreach to the poor from the perspective of the Black poor. Many Third World countries have problems with Cone's understanding of blackness, and even his talk about the ontological dimensions of blackness does not translate to poor and Third World countries. Because of these limits, notions of solidarity are understood within the context of ethnic identity of the American Black. Cone includes Asian, Caribbean, and African countries within his purview of what could become possible in terms of liberation. How will this be possible if African Americans treat Third World people the way White people treat them? The way forward is to posit solidarity with difference as a hermeneutical key. This means that we begin with a theology of difference. Solidarity must include the key of difference and explore ways to affirm that Third World people do not have to become Black if blackness means to become African Americans. Perhaps one way forward is to reinterpret blackness within the interpretive key of the praxis of Jesus.

## Black Theology and the Black Church

James Cone was passionate about the Black church. In his writing and teaching he informed us that the Black church was the home of the Black experience and of Christian theology. One of his critiques of so-called White theology was that it was pagan because it rendered the Black church and Black experience invisible. A problem with White theology, according to Cone, is that White people do theology as if Black people do not exist. There was a need in the White church for liberation—to allow the gospel of Christ to become alive and embodied among the people. Cone puts it this way: "If the real Church is the people of God whose primary task is that of being Christ to the world by proclaiming the message of the gospel (*kerygma*), by rendering services of liberation (*diakonia*), and by being itself a manifestation of the nature of the new society (*koinonia*), then the empirical institutionalized white church has failed on all counts. It certainly has not rendered services of liberation to the poor. Rather, it illustrates the values of a sick society which oppresses the poor."[9]

Cone contends that a primary reason for conceiving of a Black theology was the invisibility of Black people to White theologians. He challenges White churches and their theologians to become Black, that is, to be in solidarity with the least of God's children. Cone anchors theology in Christology. One's relationship within the church should be informed by one's relationship to Christ. It is contradictory to say yes to Jesus and no to the community called church. The Christian church, then, is the community that joins Christ in the struggle to set the oppressed free. This emphasis on Christology as the essence of the church provides a point of critique of the White church and White society. Cone's relating the Black church to the wider community was not abstract and abstruse but concrete and practical. Cone preached his first sermon in his brother's church at age sixteen. The Black church provided an alternative to the contradictions he experienced in Black life. As a child growing up in the American South in the 1950s, he

9. James H. Cone, *Black Theology and Black Power* (New York: Seabury, 1969), 71.

experienced the grace of God as the possibility for growth in love and free-dom. "White people did everything in their power to define black reality, to tell us who we were—and their definition, of course, extended no further than their social, political, and economic interests. They tried to make us believe that God created Black people to be white people's servants."[10] In this society the Black man was called "boy" and the Black woman "auntie." His mother worked as a maid in White people's homes, and his father was a janitor. It was in the Black church that the respect stolen from Black people was restored.

It has become clear that one of the major problems Cone had with the White church was that its practice of community was exclusionary. Black theology transcends the exclusionary character of the White church/theol-ogy by making the community of the oppressed normative for the church. It is this community to which Black theology is accountable and responsive. Quite often when Cone refers to the Black community, he speaks specifi-cally to the community of the oppressed. This means that the "God of the Oppressed" is not merely the God of Black people as a racial unit but is the God of all people who are in solidarity with the oppressed. It is in this sense that the church is called to become Black. Cone writes:

> It is the job of the Church to become black with him [Christ] and accept
> the shame which white society places on blacks. But the Church knows
> that what is shame to the world is holiness to God. Black is holy, that is,
> it is a symbol of God's presence in history on behalf of the oppressed. . . .
> Where there is black, there is oppression; but blacks can be assured that
> where there is blackness, there is Christ who has taken on blackness so
> that what is evil in men's eyes might become good. Therefore, Christ is
> black because he is oppressed, and oppressed because he is black. And if
> the Church is to join Christ by following his opening, it too must go where
> suffering is and become black also.[11]

10. James H. Cone, *God of the Oppressed* (New York, Seabury, 1975), 2.
11. Cone, *Black Theology and Black Power*, 69.

## The Mission of the Church

The church as community and the centrality of Christ as its reason for being point to the importance of the church's vocation as mission. Cone is insistent that the church's mission is inextricably linked to the mission of Christ. To speak of the mission of the church is at the same time to talk about the meaning Christ has for the "oppressed blacks of the land." Theology for the sake of doing theology is inadequate to meet the needs of the least of God's children. "It is one thing to assert that he is the essence of the Christian gospel, and quite another to specify the meaning of his existence in relation to the slave ships that appeared on American shores. Unless his existence is analyzed in the light of the oppressed of the land, we are still left wondering what his presence means for the auction block, the Underground Railroad and contemporary expressions of Black Power. . . . If Christ is to have any meaning for us he must leave the security of the suburbs."[12]

Cone makes it clear that theology that takes the sociological and political situation of the oppressed of the land seriously cannot be committed primarily to academic theology—the probing of the doctrines of ecclesiology and Christology for the sake of investigating their logical consistency and cogency. Theology that has Christ as its point of departure must take seriously the question, "Who is Jesus Christ for us today?" Theology must be related to life, as oppressed people who have experienced the absurdities of life seek to investigate the meaning of Christ for their situation. The liberation of the oppressed is a continuation of the ministry of Jesus in their situation. Jesus's past is the clue to his presence and activity with the oppressed. Jesus's history becomes the medium through which he is made accessible to victims. The key for unlocking the question "Who is Jesus for us today?" is found in the historical kernel of the faith. The risen Messiah is the crucified Christ. Faith and history blend and merge as the gospel story affirms that Christ came to teach us how to be human. Black theology begins with the history of Jesus as

12. James H. Cone, *A Black Theology of Liberation* (Maryknoll, NY: Orbis Books, 2005), 198–99.

the point of departure for Christian faith. The starting point is Christology from below. However, it is the interplay between the church's understanding of the history of Jesus and its understanding of the Christ of faith that provides a creative tension in which the church's mission is nurtured. The church does not have to choose between the Jesus of history and the Christ of faith. The Black church has always affirmed the Jesus of history as the Christ of faith. What this means, among other things, is that the Black church does not have to choose between a Christology "from below" and a Christology "from above," but rather the Black church keeps both in dialectical tension, acknowledging "that Christ's meaning for us today is found in our encounter with the historical Jesus as the Crucified and Risen Lord who is present with us in the struggle for freedom."[13]

According to Cone, as Christology informs the mission of the church, it must take with renewed seriousness both the *wasness* and the *isness* of Jesus. The *wasness* is Christology's point of departure as it points to the inseparable unity of Christ with victims. The *isness* calls attention to the present involvement of Christ in the struggle of victims for liberation. As the church witnesses to the power of Christ's presence in their community, it is led to ask: "What manner of man is this?"

Someone may reply:

> He is my helper in times of distress.
> He is the one that's been good to me.
> He gave me victory, the Son of the Almighty God we serve.[14]

The Black community survived the atrocities of slavery and the lynching and brutalities meted out to them by slave masters and a vicious system of slavery because of their confidence that Christ was not merely a historical figure of first-century Palestine, but he was active within their community. With this claim as backdrop, the Black church affirms its vocation to pro-

---

13. Cone, *God of the Oppressed*, 121.
14. Cone, *God of the Oppressed*, 121.

claim Jesus Christ as "God's power unto salvation." In this confidence the oppressed are called upon to live as free persons, because "sin no longer has dominion over them." The gospel of liberation is the content of the gospel of Christ through the outpouring of the Holy Spirit.

With the influence of womanist theology, which we highlighted earlier, Black theology has affirmed the importance of institutions and structures of oppression being challenged in the power of the gospel. Black theology affirms the mission of the church as being focused not only on the conversion of individuals but also on the challenging of structures that alienate and keep God's children in poverty and in enmity against God and others. The church through its mission and ministry must address powers such as racism, sexism, poverty, classism, homophobia, and social and economic exploitation that thwart the life of God's children.

## Church as Agent of Social Transformation

We observed that for James Cone the church as community of the oppressed and the church's mission to the least of God's children cannot be separated from the mission of Christ. Now we note the imperative that the church serve as agent of transformation.

A cardinal tenet of Black theology is that transformation is constitutive of the nature of the church. Transformation that results from the in-breaking of God's reign is joined to the eschatological grounding of hope as a basis for the politics of liberation. To search for the meaning of Christian hope is to conjoin hope with the politics of liberation. Political praxis serves as the main key for the church's engagement with the world. Hope then is more than the anticipation of liberation. It is both the motive force and the shape of human liberation. The vision of the eschatological reign of God makes the community of the oppressed dissatisfied with reality as they know it and provides the courage for them "to turn the world upside down." To be in the realm of God means to live with two warrants at once. On the one hand, it means accepting God's grace and being willing to give up everything for this grace. This is the meaning of repentance—*metanonia*. On the other hand, it means fighting for the creation of a new world. This is necessary because the Christ who is at work in the Black church is not the "Christ of culture" but the "Christ who transforms culture." "The event of the kingdom today is the liberation struggle in the black community. It is where people are suffering and dying for want of human dignity. It is thus incumbent upon all to see the event for what it is—God's kingdom. This is what conversion means. Black people are being converted because they see in the events around them the coming of the Lord and will not be scared into closing their eyes to it."[15]

The new future that the coming reign of God announces begins with a transformation of the present conditions that hold the oppressed community in bondage. Hope then within the community of the oppressed must become historical activity and issue forth in concrete acts of liberation in the here and now. When Black people spoke of heaven, they pointed toward a radical eschatological vision in which the community of the oppressed shares the hope and possibility of bringing into existence a new social order in which values such as justice, love, forgiveness, kindness, and integrity find full expression.

Heaven had a double meaning for Black people. For some, heaven referred to the realization of this-worldly goals such as freedom or the reality of freedom in the here and now. For Harriet Tubman, heaven meant reaching the North after helping enslaved persons to escape from the American South. After reaching free territory during the time of slavery, Tubman said:

> I looked at my hands, to see if I was the same person now I was free. There was such a glory over everything, the sun came like gold through the trees, and over the fields, and I felt like I was in heaven.
>
> I had crossed the line of which I had so long been dreaming. I was free; but there was no one to welcome me to the land of freedom. I was a stranger in a strange land, and my home after all was down in the old cabin quarter, with the old folks, and my brothers and sisters. But to this solemn

15. Cone, *A Black Theology of Liberation*, 222.

resolution I came; I was free, and they should be free also; I would bring them all there. Oh, how I prayed then, lying all alone on the cold, damp ground; "O dear Lord," I said, "I aint' got no friend but you. Come to my help, Lord, for I'm in trouble!"[16]

For Cone and Tubman, eschatology had become social and political action aimed at the creation of a new social order. This unwillingness of Tubman to rend asunder what God had joined together—the eschatological and the concrete historical—which characterizes the Black spiritual ethos, is what uniquely equipped the Black church in its long march toward freedom and liberation. The Black church became not only the symbol of the coming future reign of God but also the agent of social liberation for Black people. According to Cone, it was the encounter of Black Christians with the crucified and risen Savior that provided the inspirational source and sustaining power for the community of the oppressed as they sought to change the social, economic, and political foundations of society. Cone stated: "Christ's salvation is liberation; there is no liberation without Christ. Both meanings are inherent in the statement that Jesus Christ is the ground of human liberation. Any statement that divorces salvation from liberation or makes human freedom independent of divine freedom must be rejected."[17]

### Is Black Faith Adequate as a Tool of Analysis?

Does faith need something more in its analysis of the structures of oppression? Does the gospel have within it the tools to help oppressed people analyze evils such as racism, classism, poverty, sexism, homophobia, and ageism? Cone concludes that faith needs something more and proffers Marxism as an aspect of the more that faith needs. Marxism, he contends, should not be cursorily dismissed because it helps Black theology focus on and ques-

16. Randall C. Bailey and Jacquelyn Grant, eds., *The Recovery of Black Presence: An Interdisciplinary Exploration* (Nashville: Abingdon, 1995), 129.
17. Cone, *God of the Oppressed*, 141.

tion the social context in which the church seeks meaning making. Further, Marxism helps oppressed people understand that White theology tells them more about the theologians and their culture than it tells them about God. White theology reflects the dominant culture. Hence the ruling ideas reflect the material relationships of the dominant culture. This observation is a breakthrough for Black people, claims Cone, because it forces Black theology to consider the role of economics and politics in the definition of truth.

Sociology then becomes the midwife of Black theology. Theology is able, with the help of sociology, to question who owns the means of production and to what extent the poverty of the poor is contrived. Black theology begins to discover that the social arrangement of society reflects the interests of the dominant class and race. It is in this light that White theology and various iterations of religion serve as a sedative for the oppressed, preventing them from questioning the social and material arrangements of society. Religion often makes the oppressed comfortable in their misery and poverty. Cone writes:

> The importance of Marx for our purposes is his insistence that thought has no independence from social existence. In view of his convincing assertion that "consciousness can never be anything else than conscious existence," theologians must ask, "what is the connection between dominant material relations and the ruling ideas of a given society?" And even if they do not accept the rigid causality of so-called orthodox Marxism, theologians will find it hard to avoid the truth that their thinking about things divine is closely intertwined with the "manifestations of actual life." A serious encounter with Marx will make theologians confess their limitations, their inability to say anything about God that is not at the same time a statement about the social context of their existence.[18]

In an attempt to answer the important question, Does faith need something more?, Cone suggests that faith needs a social theory to help faith

18. Cone, *God of the Oppressed*, 42–43.

analyze the structures of oppression and thereby expose evil. Although Cone finds the Marxist analysis of capitalism and social consciousness helpful, he is not uncritical of Marxist thought, nor does he believe it is adequate as a critical tool for Black theology. "I reject dogmatic Marxism that reduces every contradiction to class analysis and thus ignores racism as a legitimate point of departure in the process of liberation. There are racist Marxists as there are racist capitalists, and we must struggle against both."[19]

Black theology does not find it necessary to exclude Marxist analysis, but coupled with Marxism must be the works of W. E. B. Du Bois, Malcolm X, Martin Luther King Jr., Sojourner Truth, Harriet Tubman, Daniel Payne, and David Walker. Cone credits King for joining social transformation and eschatology. King gave the church a vision of what it was called to become as he insisted that transformation should not take place only outside the church but also within. "If people have no dreams they will accept the world as it is and will not seek to change it. . . . No one in our time expressed this eschatological note more clearly than Martin Luther King, Jr."[20]

But to dream is not enough. Eschatology must be coupled with social analysis. This was one of the lasting contributions of King to Black theology. He insisted that unless dreams were analyzed, they would vanish into the night.

It is precisely at this point that Jesus of Nazareth becomes crucial for the Black community, because Black theology claims that in the life, death, and resurrection of Jesus of Nazareth there is an unprecedented disclosure of who we are as a people and who we are called to become. It is from the perspective of Jesus of Nazareth that the community of faith needs to understand itself. The humanity of our community resides in Jesus Christ. Jesus did not come among us in order to teach us how to be divine but to help us restore our humanity and live as children of God with each other.

---

19. See James Cone, "Black Theology and the Black Church: Where Do We Go from Here?" in *Black Theology: A Documentary History, 1966–1979*, ed. Gayraud Wilmore and James Cone (Maryknoll, NY: Orbis Books, 1979), 358.

20. Cone, "Black Theology," 353.

Black theology asserts two christological moments that are of first importance for our life together. The first is the history of Jesus, in which he identified with the "wretched of the earth" in his dying between two thieves on a hill far away. In life and in death Jesus identified with crucified peoples.

The second christological moment asserts that through cross and resurrection, Christ is no longer limited by time and space to victims in a particular place, space, ethnicity, class, gender, or race. But through the power of the resurrection, Christ identifies with victims in all places and in all walks of life. "To encounter him, the resurrected and exalted Christ who now is present in the Holy Spirit, is to encounter the possibilities and certainties of human existence which transcend the value structures of oppressive societies."[21] Christ through the power of his presence empowers the community of the oppressed to rebel against all that would encroach against its identity as daughters and sons of God. This is the beginning of liberation in the community called church as the last are first and the first are last.

21. Cone, *Black Theology and Black Power*, 211.

# Black Lives Matter

In their important book *The Birth of African-American Culture*, Sidney Mintz and Richard Price argue that Black lives have always mattered to Black people in the African diaspora. Their underlying thesis is that suffering engendered by Africans on slave ships plying the Black Atlantic created an unbreakable bond among Africans. Even though Black people hailed from different regions and tribes in Africa, some aspects of African culture were nonetheless universal—respect for the dead, confidence in ancestors in the daily affairs of life, coupled with notions of a supreme being who was not involved in everyday life but was represented by assistants, ancestors, and lesser deities. Mintz and Price contend that this view of the supreme deity made Christianity accessible to Africans in the diaspora as they began to view Jesus, the Holy Spirit, saints, and angels as emissaries of the High God assigned to fulfill his will. Further, several points of contact served as a bond for community building, as African peoples made their way through New World slavery to the African diaspora; their love of music (especially drumming), religion, and prayer and their belief in a world peopled by spirits were of first importance. An added dimension was the experience of enslaved Africans being shackled together as they crossed the Black Atlantic, on their journey to the New World. This experience of being shackled together and squeezed into the same cramped space formed a bond among Africans. This was the case among members of the same sex, as men and women were separated on the voyage.

Africans who recognized each other on this common journey referred to each other as "shipmates." Mintz and Price regard this bonding among Africans on their voyage into plantation slavery as the beginning of inter-American relationships.

The Middle Passage was not merely a negative experience, since enslaved persons were not passive onboard slave ships. In the wake of dehumanization and humiliation, enslaved persons reached out to each other and formed a social-bonding network that may be traced in contexts as different as Trinidad, Suriname, Jamaica, and the United States. "The bond between shipmates, those who shared passage on the same slaver, is the most striking example. In widely scattered parts of Afro-America, the 'shipmate' relationship became a major principle of social organization and continued for decades and even centuries to shape ongoing social relationships."[1] In Jamaica, the term "shipmate" was transposed to "brother" or "sister" and was regarded as a most affectionate and endearing term. "In Suriname . . . the equivalent term 'sippi' was at first used between people who actually shared the experience of transport in a single vessel: later, it began to be used between two slaves who belonged to a single plantation, preserving the essential notion of fellow sufferers who have a special bond."[2] Over the years the term "sippi," "brother" or "shipmate," has been used among members of the African diasporan community as a term of endearment for fellow members of the community who find themselves in similar circumstances of misfortune. The appeal of this term of endearment had its genesis on the journey from Africa to the New World and was another way of saying "Black lives matter." We are in this together. We are here for each other. The term "shipmate" signals the importance of Black faith among Africa's children forging an identity in a strange land among strange people.

When it is remembered that slave ships often docked in the Caribbean ports and provided an occasion for enslaved people to be acculturated to plantation life prior to their journey and introduction to plantation life in the colonies on the American mainland, the term "shipmates" (brothers and sisters) is both symbolically and literally true in relation to Afro-Caribbean and African American people. This calling each other "shipmate," "sippi," or "brother and sister" was Black people's way to remember the journey from freedom to slavery. It was Black people's way to remember Africa.

The memory of Africa became a controlling metaphor and organizing principle in the New World as Black people encountered the harsh and hege-

---

1. Sidney W. Mintz and Richard Price, *The Birth of African-American Culture: An Anthropological Perspective* (Boston: Beacon, 1992), 43.
2. Mintz and Price, *The Birth of African-American Culture*, 43–44.

monic conditions imposed on them by plantation slavery. By recalling their journey from freedom to slavery, they were reminded that Black lives matter, as the memory of ancestors, and a sense of their presence (spirits), empowered them to create spaces for worship in forests or brush harbors down by the riverside. The Black community's memory of Africa and their affirmation of each other created sites for dreaming and forging a new consciousness. The awakening of a new consciousness engendered by the memory of Africa and the embrace of community even in the teeth of slavery became the basis for the creation of the Black church. C. Eric Lincoln frames the issue for us: "The black Christians in white churches were cramped in their style and stifled by the requirements of racial conformity. Though they were formally 'in church,' it was demonstrably not 'their' church, a communication that spoke pointedly and consistently through the sermons, the prayers, the spiritual suppression, and the absence of fellowship. In the white churches the Africans were offered a God who had cursed them and ordained their travail and debasement in perpetuity. . . . Hence, it was inevitable that Black Christians would heed the call to 'come ye out from among them.'"[3]

This certainly cuts across the notion of shipmates, as Black lives were not valued. Black people were not accorded the respect due to God's children. The Christian church was a space in which Black people were often humiliated and denied fellowship. Africa's children were in church, but it was not their church, it was a church in which God had cursed them, according to Lincoln. This devaluing of Black life was a consequence of the system of New World slavery. On arrival in the New World, Africans were sold as human cargo and became enslaved, owned and controlled by the master class. Throughout the region, drumming, dancing, and religious practices that remembered Africa were forbidden. Enslaved persons were forbidden to use their own language or to give their children African names. The master class devised various means to erase the memory of Africa. As the African priest/medicine man/medicine woman emerged on plantations throughout

---

3. C. Eric Lincoln, introduction to *Mighty like a River*, by Andrew Billingsley (New York: Oxford University Press, 2003), xxi.

the New World, Christians believed that the antidote to African ways and practices, indeed to African religion, was to baptize the African priest. It was widely believed by the master class that baptism would neutralize the gifts of the African healer. In many cases, enslaved people were baptized by European clergy before boarding the ship, or on deck as the ship set sail through the Middle Passage en route to plantations in the Caribbean at first, and later to the American mainland. The practice of baptizing enslaved persons was used to justify slavery by arguing that a Christian slave is to be preferred to a heathen infidel, even if that infidel is free. It was in this context that Orlando Patterson pointed out that one of the underlying issues in slavery was the imbalance of power, relations of inequality, or domination in which the world of the master as it intersected with that of the enslaved person was one in which the master class exercised total control and power over the enslaved. "Slavery is one of the most extreme forms of the relation of domination, approaching the limits of total power from the viewpoint of the master, and of total powerlessness from the viewpoint of the slave."[4] According to Patterson, the master-slave relation was based on violence and would not survive without violence. Profit was the goal of the master class, and violence was the means by which it enacted and extracted labor. There was no plantation, however generous the master, in which the whip (violence) did not at least serve as threat. "In his powerlessness the slave became an extension of his master's power. He was a human surrogate, recreated by his master with god-like power in his behalf. . . . Without the master the slave does not exist. . . . All persons are created by God, the slave is created by Tuareg (master)."[5] It is quite clear that Patterson seeks to emphasize that the enslaved person was a dominated being, one whose body belonged to the master. Patterson underscores this in his notion of natal alienation—the loss of family, both extended and immediate. "Alienated from all 'rights' or claims of birth, [the slave] ceased to belong in his own right to any legitimate social

4. Orlando Patterson, "The Constituent Elements of Slavery," in *Caribbean Slavery in the Atlantic World*, ed. Verene Shepherd and Hilary McD. Beckles (Kingston, Jamaica: Ian Randle Publishers, 2000), 32.

5. Patterson, "The Constituent Elements of Slavery," 34.

order. . . . Slaves differed from other human beings in that they were not allowed freely to integrate the experience of their ancestors into their lives, to inform their understanding of social reality with the inherited meanings of their natural forebears."[6] Patterson was right in insisting that the master class sought to deny Black people their heritage but could not deny them their history in their attempt to erase the memory of Africa. Black people were denied human value. Black people were sold from the auction block like horses, cows, and cotton. They had no control of their lives or of their children. Black people were for sale. Black lives did not matter.

## Black Resistance

Black people offered resistance not only through revolts, running away, and insurrections but also by calling on their ancestors for help when they felt Black lives were devalued. Enslaved people remembered Africa, and Africa became a controlling metaphor of liberation. "In Puerto Rico some black women were imprisoned for practicing witch-craft and spiritualism under the government of Gabriel de Roxas (1608–14). Archbishop Cristobal Rodriguez y Suarez reported yet another case. Witch-craft and other types of black magic had been observed and punished since 1610 by the court of inquisition of Cartagena de Indias."[7] Christian churches made it clear that their primary concern was with saving the souls of enslaved persons and not disrupting plantation life. When the church baptized the bodies of enslaved persons, it was with the understanding that they would be received into a community that sacralized the system and structure of slavery, and with the hope that baptism would make the enslaved more gentle and diligent, and more obedient to the demands of the planter class. The miracle was that "despite those persecution measures, African slaves succeeded in keeping their own reli-

---

6. Patterson, "The Constituent Elements of Slavery," 34.

7. Charles Joiner, " Believer I Know: The Emergence of African-American Christianity," in *African American Christianity*, ed. Paul E. Johnson (Berkeley: University of California Press, 1994), 48–49.

gious world. Uprooted from their homeland, they maintained some of their identity and so filled the vacuum to which the church only paid attention in an inadequate way."[8] Frederick Douglass summed up the way a majority of enslaved persons viewed Christianity—with suspicion—as a religion of the oppressors. Although they gave it nominal attention and saw elements of freedom in the Bible and its liturgy, they were willing to mix Christianity with the veneration of the ancestors and the spirit they encountered in the natural world, be it in the forest, in animals, or in streams. This begins to explain why enslaved persons placed more faith in an African interpretation of Christianity than in the missionaries' articulation of Christianity. The bottom line for African peoples ensnared in the throes of slavery was whether or not Christianity affirmed that Black lives mattered. Black people were forced to carve out liberative space on the journey into freedom.

According to Williams, we cannot with certainty say the Black church is here and not there. Wherever Black lives are being transformed and women and men are agitating for freedom, the church is present. Williams taught us the importance of experiencing history from the perspective of victims rather than through the ideologies of the ruling class. Black theology affirms that theology must spring from the soil of human suffering. This points to the priority of the Black/womanist experience and its call to celebrate Black bodies. In a context and culture in which Black bodies are bought and sold, and in which the church teaches that the soul belongs to God while the body belongs to the master class, Black theology must teach that body and soul belong together. As theology affirms the inseparability of body and soul, liberation must include healing and restoration of humiliated bodies. Bodies are also in need of healing.

While it is clear that Martin Luther King Jr. was on the right course in his advocacy of the Beloved Community, in which all would be accepted as sons and daughters of God, the current emergency situation in which young Black men and women are often killed by the police and the prison

8. Joiner, "Believer I Know," 49.

population is over 40 percent Black and people of color, the first order of
business in Black theology ought to be the creation of a social and political
context in which Black lives are regarded as meaningful. Black theologians
regard King as a mentor who articulated an agenda of healing in the community. However, Black theology must begin to ask whether King's vision of
the Beloved Community should be regarded as an eschatological possibility,
that which will happen in God's time, perhaps at the end of history. But
as eschatology—the vision of God's love and purpose for humanity—cuts
into and informs history, Black theology highlights the divine presence in
the community of the oppressed. Truth about who we are and who we are
called to become is given in the community of the oppressed. Theology in
a racist, class-structured, patriarchal, and homophobic society must not
reduce people to abstractions but must take them seriously and affirm them
as daughters and sons of God who are valued. We must begin with black
bodies that learn, play, struggle for meaning, and often are set aside by a
dominant culture that does not affirm their value. One of the important
assets of Cone's emphasis on the Black experience as point of departure for
Black theology is that it attributes value to the Black community and does
not look outside the Black community for affirmation. The Black experience refuses to value self only in the light of other selves that are outside
the Black community. This, I believe, could be understood as one of the
fundamental flaws of King's insistence of a community of selves that reside
outside the Black community as a frame of reference for the valuing and
flourishing of Black people. King's insistence on his notion of mutuality
of being, an interdependence of being that is crucial for Black well-being,
raises the specter and allows the possibility of other communities holding
Black well-being hostage.

One problem with life lived in a White racist society is that perhaps the
only space—the only place where Black persons may be assured of their
somebodiness—is in the Black community. The Black frame of reference
becomes the only space where the promise of Black existence flourishing
outweighs the threat of self-hate and rejection by the other.

CHAPTER 7

**Original Sin**

Because King had come to understand White supremacy and Black inferiority as the root cause of "original sin" in America, he came to recognize that the Beloved Community he proffered was a part of the idealized self of which he dreamed. King did not give up on the Beloved Community, but he began to see clearly that in a racist society and world the Black experience was an important emergency door for the Black community. King's call for Black people to unify and pool resources was not an attempt to abolish notions of the Beloved Community, but it was a way of asking: What does it say about us as community when the most vulnerable among us are allowed to be the point of departure for reflection and praxis in communities of reconciliation?

King, in the light of the crisis that ultimately took his life on April 4, 1968, posited a new center for talk about restored community. The center was no longer an integrated self/community; the Black experience would serve as the center of a conceptual framework. Since King was a systematic theologian by training, it is appropriate to suggest that this may be a way to talk about cross and resurrection within the framework of Beloved Community. King's attempt to decenter the idealized self and place emphasis on the existential self as point of departure for his vision of the Beloved Community is another way of talking about cross and resurrection. King saw the Beloved Community as the restored and redeemed community that had overcome racism and its varied forms of oppression. The Beloved Community was to emerge out of the ashes of racism and would lay to rest segregated existence in the United States of America and beyond. The suffering engendered by the civil rights movement—persons being killed by lynch mobs and overzealous police, hundreds imprisoned, and in the end, even the leader being assassinated—was the price of redemptive suffering that was prerequisite for the resurrected form of the Beloved Community.

What the strike by sanitation workers helped King to see was that his dream of the Beloved Community was the dream of the idealized self. It was the dream of the resurrected and restored community. While King could not give up on the dream of resurrection, he had to confront the reality of the cross, not just as an event that happened two thousand years ago when Jesus Christ was crucified but as a necessary part of the American experience.

The cross has always been at the very heart of the Black experience. Struggling with blackness and the pain it engenders is a very heavy cross. What makes the cross our cross is that it is the cross of Christ. It is interesting that in the early church Christians were called the people of the cross. Powered by the Black experience, members of Black churches often inquire, "Who is this Jesus who knows all about our troubles? Who is this Jesus who sees all our troubles?" This Jesus is the crucified one, who was killed and buried, and who rose again for the liberation of sons and daughters of God. Through Jesus, God enters into solidarity with all who are oppressed and heavy-laden. Through Jesus, God announces that the children of God are not called on to suffer as much as possible, but because of his suffering, we can begin to move into the resurrection realm where there is resistance to injustice and all forms of oppression. Through the symbol of the cross we can affirm that Black lives are valued as we join Christ protesting against the unjust suffering and are willing to share in the suffering of Christ in the world as a way to transformation of this world. Through resurrection Jesus makes possible liberation for victims and empowers Blacks and all who are victimized to shout from rooftops that Black lives matter because they are valued by the community of the oppressed.

**The Way Forward**

At the end of the day, Black faith announces that in spite of human frailty and sin, the community of the oppressed is in God's hands and God will not fail us. Black faith affirms the Son of God, Jesus Christ, to be in solidarity with poor and oppressed victims. The form Christ takes in the world today is clear—it is the Black community; those who are persecuted because of their lowly status and set aside because of the color of their skin find refuge and solace in Jesus. In the valley of deepest darkness Black people would sing—"Nobody knows the trouble I've seen. Nobody knows my sorrow."

"Nobody knows the trouble I've seen. Glory, Hallelujah." Jesus was their companion, and the source of "Glory, Hallelujah." There was an indissoluble relationship between the Black community and Christ. Earlier we noted that Africans in the New World, when introduced to the Christian ways of thinking by the missionary, would envision Jesus as one of the spirits to turn to especially in times of travail and pain. For many Jesus was their favorite spirit. However, if Jesus was unable to meet their needs, or answer in a timely way, they would turn to other spirits. Cone signifies this way of thinking in suggesting that what makes Jesus special and indispensable to the Black community is his solidarity with Black reality.

> The Black community is an oppressed community primarily because of its blackness; hence the Christological importance of Jesus must be found in his blackness. If he is not black as we are, then the resurrection has little significance for our times. Indeed, if he cannot be what we are, we cannot be who he is. Our being with him is dependent on his being with us in the oppressed black community, revealing to us what is necessary for our liberation. The definition of Jesus as black is crucial for Christology if we truly believe in his continued presence today.[9]

The bottom line for Cone is that only a Jew could redeem Judaism and only a Black Christ can save the Black community. Black faith is emphatic, Black lives matter, and if the risen Christ is not Black, and in solidarity with Black people, he is rendered irrelevant, and racism, sexism, classism, and grinding poverty and high rates of incarceration of members of the Black community will continue unabated. The Jewishness of Jesus leads Black faith to assert that only a Black Christ in solidarity with the Black community can become the source of healing and salvation. The existen-

---

9. James H. Cone, *A Black Theology of Liberation*, fortieth anniversary ed. (Maryknoll, NY: Orbis Books, 2010), 126.

tial situation is an emergency in which the alarms are sounding forth and the Black community cannot trust the White community to interpret the meaning of the resurrected Christ for us. Carina Ray illustrates the emergency situation.

> "If I go, could they kill me too?" my 9-year old asked. His question hung in the air like thick fog. Local activists had organized a caravan protest against police brutality in our small town in upstate New York, and I thought my son would be eager to join. . . . We joined the rear of the long caravan and my son asked, "Can I roll down the window and yell, 'Black Lives matter'?" The next morning, I came down to the breakfast table to find him tracing a black-power fist. . . . "Mom!" he shouted about half an hour later. "I can't find their last words!" I sat down next to him and saw that he had written "I can't breathe" followed by George Floyd's name . . . and "I can't breathe" followed by Eric Garner's name. . . . Over the next hour we searched the internet but found only what are believed to be Sandra Bland's last words . . . and Michael Brown's. . . . When we got to Tamir Rice, the 12-year-old-boy in Cleveland who was gunned down by a white police officer, I said: "Tamir is why I don't ever let you play with toy guns. Black kids don't get the benefit of the doubt."[10]

Carina Ray, with empathy and compassion, illustrates the emergency situation in which Black theology questions whether four hundred years of slavery, racism, grinding poverty, and death will be removed by Christ's triumph of grace and resurrection. To paraphrase Cone, If Christ does not affirm that Black lives matter, can we trust him?

The challenge confronting us in the invitation to become Black with Christ and to affirm that Black lives matter is to enter into solidarity with the least of God's children. The invitation to the reign of God is to transformation and liberation of the private self to participate in the corporate selfhood

10. Carina Ray, "'Could the Police Kill Me, Too?' My Young Son Asked Me," *New York Times*, June 20, 2020, 2, https://www.nytimes.com/2020/06/20/opinion/sunday/george -floyd-protests-black.html.

of Christ. "If anyone is in Christ, there is a new creation: everything old has passed away; see, everything has become new!" (1 Cor. 5:17).

> Martin Luther King often referred at the end of his sermons to a Black hymn which goes back to a lamentation of the prophet Jeremiah. Jeremiah saw how the evil were successful and the good had to suffer. "Is there no balm in Gilead?" he asked, "is there no longer a physician there?" (8.22). Cone writes:

>> Centuries later, it was our enslaved forebears who experienced the injustice of life, and who day in and day out expected nothing but the whip of the overseer, endless cottonfields, and incredible heat; but in this situation they did something quite astonishing: they looked back a few centuries and transformed Jeremiah's questions of his time into a sign of rebellion. Now they could sing:

>>> There is a balm in Gilead
>>> To make the wounded whole
>>> there is a balm in Gilead
>>> to heal the sinsick soul.[11]

As the oppressed begin to transform situations of suffering into expressions of Black faith marked by confidence in the divine, they begin to construct a new future with songs of healing in Gilead and of freedom to embrace their reality as sons and daughters of God. Through their encounter with the biblical text, and the spirit of God, they affirm that Black lives matter, as they rob suffering and sin of ultimacy, throw off the shackles of oppression, and join God in the work of liberation. We join the chorus with oppressed people, "For freedom Christ has set us free. Stand firm, therefore, and do not submit again to the yoke of slavery" (Gal. 5:1).

11. Dorothee Sölle, *Thinking about God: An Introduction to Theology* (Harrisburg, PA: Trinity Press International, 1990), 100–101.

———————————————

# Linking Faith and Salvation

On both sides of the Black Atlantic enslaved persons were able to recognize notions of sin and sacrifice because there were parallels in their own religions. In the Caribbean during the era of slavery enslaved persons acknowledged that human beings are sinful but do not self-define as sinners. Christian faith, in several iterations, taught that human beings who were estranged from God were lost and held in contempt by God. They were on their way to hell and therefore in need of divine salvation. African Americans were taught to acknowledge sinfulness, divine contempt, and the desire to be accepted through the love and sacrifice of Jesus. Jesus was often seen as one of the lesser deities who mediated between the human condition of sinfulness and the divine gift of grace and mercy.

One way the church kept Black people in their place as unequal to White people was by teaching that a terrible sense of worthlessness and unworthiness came with one's relationship to Jesus. In the act of viewing Jesus as worthy, one saw oneself as unworthy, and condemned in that state until the church mediated divine forgiveness and grace. The journey to divine acceptance was not automatic. Richard Allen, the founder of Bethel Methodist Church, illustrates the sense of unworthiness that accompanied a relationship with Jesus: "I was awakened and brought to see myself, poor, wretched, and undone, and without the mercy of God. . . . I cried to the Lord both night and day. . . . All of a sudden my dungeon shook, my chains flew off, and glory to God I cried. My soul was filled. I cried enough—for me the savior died."[1] He went on to found a church and became a leader of his people.

Life for enslaved persons in the New World was an existential expression of bondage from which they sought freedom, and religion provided the impetus and means for this sought-after deliverance.

1. Albert J. Raboteau, *A Fire in the Bones* (Boston: Beacon, 1995), 81.

The movement of great numbers of Africans to the Caribbean first and then later to US colonies was inspired by the Christian church. In his celebrated work *The History, Civil and Commercial, of the British Colonies in the West Indies,* Bryan Edwards, the eighteenth-century historian, informs us that in 1517 Charles V of Spain granted permission for four thousand Black people to be brought annually to the islands of Hispaniola, Cuba, Jamaica, and Puerto Rico. The emperor granted this request because of the pleading of the church. Edwards states: "The concurrence of the emperor to this measure was obtained at the solicitation of Bartholomew de las Casas, Bishop of Chiapa, the celebrated protector of the Indians; and the conduct of this great prelate on that occasion has been the subject of much censure. . . . While he contended . . . for the liberation of the people born in one quarter of the globe, he labored to enslave the inhabitants of another region and in the warmth and zeal to save the Americans from the yoke, pronounced it to be lawful and expedient to impose one, still heavier on the Africans."[2]

The basis of the church's action was called into question then, and today the church must continue to question the norms for its action. Is God's action in Jesus Christ the source of faith and salvation? The action of the church as evidenced in Bishop Bartholomew de las Casas's stance against Black people calls into question God's love for the least of God's children. Black faith as the praxis of Jesus makes clear that God in Christ does not condone slavery and oppression. The sad reality is that the church's action through its bishop makes the church complicit for the presence of Black people in the Caribbean, their enslavement, their abuse, and their difficult struggle to affirm their worth as sons and daughters of God.

The unfolding of the history of the abuse of Black people in the New World brings to the fore a question historian Bryan Edwards broaches when he asks: How may we talk about the love of God in the context of oppression? The action of the church coupled with the question raised by Edwards

2. Bryan Edwards, *The History, Civil and Commercial, of the British Colonies in the West Indies,* vol. 1 (London: Stockdale, 1801), 38–39. Bartholomew de las Casas (1474–1566), who was in many ways the father of Caribbean theology, was a contemporary of Martin Luther and John Calvin.

places Black people and the God of the Christian church together. Edwards suggests that the God whom the church proclaims as savior will condemn all oppressive structures. He wonders how this will be if the Christian God is held captive by the church. Edwards could not resolve this contradiction.[3] A clue to how we may talk about the love of God and oppression is found in Scripture's witness to God, who entered into a situation of oppression, so that through God's suffering, victims may come to know God as the source of salvation. A Christian interpretation of Isaiah 53 will suggest a partial answer to questions about divine love and oppression.

> He was oppressed, and he was afflicted,
>> yet he opened not his mouth;
> like a lamb that is led to the slaughter,
>> and like a sheep that before its shearers is dumb,
>> so he opened not his mouth.
> By oppression and judgment he was taken away;
>> and as for his generation, who considered
> that he was cut off out of the land of the living,
>> stricken for the transgression of my people?
> And they made his grave with the wicked
>> and with a rich man in his death,
> although he had done no violence,
>> and there was no deceit in his mouth. (Isa. 53:7–9 RSV)

In reading from Isaiah 61:1–2, Jesus interpreted his mission as being for victims of oppression (Luke 4:18–19). Martin Luther, a contemporary of Bartholomew de las Casas, stated in his *Heidelberg Disputation* that to know the love of God as it is revealed in Jesus Christ is to experience a God who is hidden in suffering: "God can only be found in suffering and the cross."[4] Therefore, Christian love proclaims that "God suffered in Jesus, God died on

---

3. Edwards, *The History*, 35–36.

4. *Selected Writings of Martin Luther, 1517–1520*, ed. Theodore G. Tappert (Philadelphia: Fortress, 1967), 79.

the cross of Christ . . . so that we may live in the future."[5] Both Luther and Jürgen Moltmann suggest that God's love revealed in Jesus does not affirm structures of death and bondage; on the contrary, God's love shows the way out of the vicious circles of death and estrangement.

Edwards did not understand that Christian love points to God, who is not only for the church but also against the church, as God stands over against the church in judgment. This seems to be the theological significance of Matthew 25:35–46. Whenever the church participates in denying people their right to be human, the church is condemned by God (Matt. 25:45–46).

The former prime minister of Jamaica, Michael Manley, in an address to the World Council of Churches, expands our understanding of oppressive conditions in which the oppressed of the land struggle for freedom and liberation. "Let me remind you that liberation is about victims. . . . Every family that is undernourished is a victim. Not only the unemployed, but every man and woman whose work is underpaid, irregular or insecure are victims. And every child born of unions of such men and women are doubly victimized; for they do not only have to suffer malnutrition, disease. . . . Every person who has been denied equality, who has been treated with less than full regard, who has been maimed or killed, because of race or religion, is a victim."[6]

The history of the abuse of Black people recounted by Manley suggests that fear of the loss of freedom to be fully human functions as a mirror through which oppressed persons see their histories reflected. A central question is, how may the oppressed restore their stolen identity and claim their status as sons and daughters of God? Gayraud Wilmore highlights the depth of the problem: "Even under the most favorable conditions, Black slavery in the New World was a deliberate system of cultural and psychological genocide. Every connection with the past was to be obliterated and the slaves were to be thoroughly dehumanized and brainwashed

5. Jürgen Moltmann, *The Crucified God* (New York: Harper & Row, 1974), 216.
6. Michael Manley, "From the Shackles of Domination and Oppression" (Address Document no. A8, World Council of Churches, Fifth Assembly, Nairobi, Kenya, 1975), 5.

that they would forget that he or she had been anything other than Nigger John or Nigger Mandy created by God, as the early slave catechisms taught, to 'make a crop.'"[7] The religious argument that God created Black people to make a crop was another way in which churches sought to rob Black people of their freedom to step into their destinies as sons and daughters of God.

One of the breakthroughs that occurred in the creation of Black sacred spaces, whether in the brush arbor or down by the riverside, was in the practice of Black faith: Black people would physically remove themselves from the cruel world constructed by the master class. In this new space-place they concluded that God meant them for freedom—God is the God of their salvation. Through Black faith they remembered Africa and were open to an African awakening. Black people began to learn that Christianity as presented by the master class or rulers had to be handled with care as it represented an agenda that was not in their best interest.

Another breakthrough for Black faith was that Black people began to read the Bible for themselves and discovered that the God of their ancestors was the God of the Bible. This allowed them to read the Bible with confidence from an African frame of reference and to regard the Bible as normative for the practice of Black faith. Cuban theologian Sergio Arce Martinez sums up for us his reading of the Gospel of Saint Luke: "Every attempt to liberate humanity from poverty, from oppression, from ignorance, from exploitation, as Jesus announced it in Nazareth naturally amounts to revolution. The revolution is destruction of the structure of slavery, but it is more than that. It is re-creation of a person who frees himself or herself from vested interests to go in search of other, more genuinely human—that is more genuinely social—interests. . . . That is the historic movement which in the language of Luke is called the year of Grace of the Lord, remembering the year of Grace of the old covenant."[8]

7. Gayraud Wilmore, "Identity Crisis: Blacks in Predominantly White Denominations," in *Colloquium on Black Religion*, ed. William Howard (New York: Reformed Church in America, 1976), 5.

8. Sergio Arce Martinez, "Christ and Liberation," *Cuba Review* 5, no. 3 (1977): 405.

In the struggle for freedom a new humanity will emerge. However, it is the presence of God in the struggle that guarantees the emergence of a new humanity.

> Yet I have been the LORD your God
>> ever since the land of Egypt;
> you know no God but me,
>> and besides me there is no savior. (Hos. 13:4)

God is our salvation. The good news is that God's freedom becomes the instrument that breaks the power of human bondage and makes possible the participation of Black faith in the creation of a new humanity.

# Selected Bibliography

Alexander, Michelle. *The New Jim Crow: Mass Incarceration in the Age of Color-blindness.* New York: New Press, 2020.

Baptist, Edward. *The Half Has Never Been Told: Slavery and the Making of American Capitalism.* New York: Basic Books, 2014.

Barrett, Leonard E. *Soul-Force: African Heritage in Afro-American Religion.* New York: Anchor Press, 1974.

Barth, Karl. *The Teaching of the Church regarding Baptism.* London: SCM, 1963.

Beasley-Murray, R. G. *Baptism Today and Tomorrow.* New York: St. Martin's, 1966.

Boothe, Hyacinth I. "A Theological Journey for an Emancipatory Theology." *Caribbean Journal of Religious Studies* 17, no. 1 (April 1966).

Braxton, Brad Ronnell. *No Longer Slaves: Galatians and African American Experience.* Collegeville, MN: Liturgical Press, 2002.

Cannon, Katie Geneva. "Transformative Grace." In *Feminist and Womanist Essays in Reformed Dogmatics*, edited by Amy Plantinga Pauw and Serene Jones. Louisville: Westminster John Knox, 2006.

Carter, Harold. *The Prayer Tradition of Black People.* Valley Forge, PA: Judson, 1966.

Cone, James H. *Black Theology and Black Power.* New York: Seabury, 1969.

———. "Black Theology and Third World Theologies." *Chicago Theological Seminary Register* 62, no. 1 (Winter 1983): 3–12.

———. *A Black Theology of Liberation.* Maryknoll, NY: Orbis Books, 2005.

———. "The Easy Conscience of America's Churches on Race." In *Spirituality and Justice*, ed. Bill Thompson. Reprint, Chicago: CTA, 2003.

———. *For My People: Black Theology and the Black Church.* Maryknoll, NY: Orbis Books, 1984.

———. *God of the Oppressed.* New York: Seabury, 1975.

———. *Martin and Malcolm and America: A Dream or a Nightmare.* Maryknoll, NY: Orbis Books, 1992.

———. *Risks of Faith: The Emergence of a Black Theology of Liberation, 1968–1998.* Boston: Beacon, 1999.

———. "What Is Christian Theology?" *Caribbean Journal of Religious Studies* 3, no. 2 (September 1980).

Cooper, Carolyn. *Noises in the Blood.* London: Macmillan, 1993.

Costas, Orlando E. *Christ outside the Gate.* Maryknoll, NY: Orbis Books, 1995.

Crawford, Elaine Brown. *Hope in the Holler: A Womanist Theology.* Louisville: Westminster John Knox, 2002.

Douglas, Kelly Brown. "Womanist Theology: What Is Its Relationship to Black Theology?" In *Black Theology: A Documentary History, 1980–1992*, edited by Gayraud Wilmore and James Cone. Vol. 2. Maryknoll, NY: Orbis Books, 1992.

———. *Stand Your Ground: Black Bodies and the Justice of God.* Maryknoll, NY: Orbis Books, 2015.

Douglass, Frederick. *The Life and Writings of Frederick Douglass.* Vol. 11, *Pre–Civil War Decade, 1850–1860.* Edited by Philip S. Foner. New York: International Publishers, 1997.

Drake, St. Clair. *The Redemption of Africa and Black Religion.* Chicago. Third World, 1970.

Edwards, Bryan. *The History, Civil and Commercial, of the British Colonies in the West Indies.* Vol. 1. London: Stockdale, 1801.

Erskine, Noel Leo. "How Do We Know What to Believe?" In *Essentials of Christian Theology*, edited by William C. Placher. Louisville: Westminster John Knox, 2003.

———. "Light from Black Theologies." In *Sources of Light: Resources for Baptist Churches Practicing Theology*, edited by Amy L. Chilton and Steven R. Harmon. Macon, GA: Mercer University Press, 2020.

Filson, Floyd V. *A Commentary of the Gospel of St. Matthew.* London: Black, 1960.

Fison, J. E. *The Blessing of the Holy Spirit.* London: Longmans, Green, 1950.

Garvey, Amy Jacques. *Garvey and Garveyism.* New York: Macmillan, 1970.

Garvey, Marcus, Jr. "Garveyism: Some Reflections on Its Significance for Today." In *Marcus Garvey and the Vision of Africa*, edited by John Henrik Clarke with assistance of Amy Jacques Garvey. Baltimore: Black Classic, 1974.

Goldman, Vivien. "Uptown Ghetto Living: Bob Marley in His Own Backyard." In *Reggae, Rasta, Revolution*, edited by Chris Potash. London: Schumer Books, 1997.

Grant, Jacquelyn. "Womanist Jesus and the Mutual Struggle for Liberation." In *The Recovery of Black Presence: An Interdisciplinary Exploration*, edited by Randall C. Bailey and Jacquelyn Grant. Nashville: Abingdon, 1995.

Hannah, Barbara Makeda Blake. *Rastafari: The New Creation*. 4th ed. Kingston, Jamaica: Masquel, 1997.

Herzog, Frederick. *Liberation Theology: Liberation in the Light of the Fourth Gospel*. New York: Seabury, 1972.

Hopkins, Dwight, and Edward P. Antonio, eds. *The Cambridge Companion to Black Theology*. Cambridge: Cambridge University Press, 2012.

Joiner, Charles. "Believer I Know: The Emergence of African American Christianity." In *African American Christianity*, edited by Paul E. Johnson. Berkeley: University of California Press, 1994.

Keck, Leander E. *Paul and His Letters*. Philadelphia: Fortress, 1988.

King, Martin L., Jr. "Remaining Awake through a Great Revolution." In *Testament of Hope: The Essential Writings of Martin Luther King Jr.*, edited by James Melvin Washington. 3rd ed. San Francisco: Harper & Row, 1986.

———. *Strength to Love*. Cleveland: Collins, 1963.

———. *Why We Can't Wait*. New York: New American Library, 1963.

La Croix, Oscar. "How the Church Conceives of Her Mission in the French West Indies." In *Out of the Depths*, edited by Idris Hamid. San Fernando, Trinidad: Rahaman Printery, 1977.

Lehmann, Paul. *Ethics in a Christian Context*. New York: Harper & Row, 1976.

Lincoln, C. Eric. Introduction to *Mighty like a River*, by Andrew Billingsley. New York: Oxford University Press, 2003.

Luther, Martin. *Selected Writings of Martin Luther, 1517–1520*. Edited by Theodore G. Tappert. Philadelphia: Fortress, 1967.

Marley, Bob. *The Complete Lyrics of Bob Marley*. Edited by Harry Hawke. London: Omnibus, 2001.

Martinez, Sergio Arce. "Evangelization and Politics from the Cuban Point of View."

In *Evangelization and Politics*, edited by Sergio Arce Martinez and Oden Marichal. New York: Circus Inc., 1982.

Middleton, Richard. "Identity and Subversion in Babylon." In *Religion, Culture, and Tradition in the Caribbean*, edited by Hemchand Gossai and Samuel Murrell. New York: St. Martin's, 2000.

Mintz, Sidney W., and Richard Price. *The Birth of African-American Culture: An Anthropological Perspective*. Boston: Beacon, 1992.

Moltmann, Jürgen. *The Crucified God*. New York: Harper & Row, 1974.

Nettleford, Rex. "Discourse on Rastafari Reality." In *Chanting Down Babylon*, edited by Nathaniel Samuel Murrell, William David Spencer, and Adrian Anthony McFarlane. Philadelphia: Temple University Press, 1998.

Nygren, Anders. *Commentary on Romans*. London: SCM, 1958.

Patterson, Orlando. "The Constituent Elements of Slavery." In *Caribbean Slavery in the Atlantic World*, edited by Verene Shepherd and Hilary McD. Beckles. Kingston, Jamaica: Ian Randle Publishers, 2000.

Phillippo, James M. *Jamaica: Its Past and Present State*. London: John Snow 1843. Reprint, Westport, CT: Negro University Press, 1970.

Raboteau, Albert J. *A Fire in the Bones*. Boston: Beacon, 1995.

Roberts, J. Deotis. *Liberation and Reconciliation: A Black Theology*. Louisville: Westminster John Knox, 2005.

Smith, Ashley. *Real Roots and Potted Plants*. Kingston, Jamaica: Mandeville Publishers, 1984.

Sölle, Dorothee. *Thinking about God: An Introduction to Theology*. Harrisburg, PA: Trinity Press International, 1990.

Stewart, Dianne. *Three Eyes for the Journey: African Dimensions of the Jamaican Religious Experience*. New York: Oxford University Press, 2005.

Taylor, Burchell K. "Caribbean Theology." *Caribbean Journal of Religious Studies* 3, no. 2 (September 1980).

Taylor, Don, and Mike Henry, eds. *Marley and Me*. Kingston, Jamaica: Kingston Publishers, 1994.

Watty, William. *From Shore to Shore: Soundings in Caribbean Theology*. Kingston, Jamaica: UTCWI Press, 1981.

Williams, Eric. *From Columbus to Castro: The History of the Caribbean, 1492–1969*. New York: Vintage Books, 1969.

———. *The Negro in the Caribbean*. New York: Negro University Press, 1942.

Wilmore, Gayraud, and James Cone, eds. *Black Theology: A Documentary History, 1966–1979*. Maryknoll, NY: Orbis Books, 1979.

# Index of Authors

# Index of Subjects

Adam, 77–78, 85
African religion, 3–5, 9–10, 177–78
atonement, 69–70, 71
awakening, Black, 27
awareness, Black, 26–28

Babylon, 48, 50
baptism: and African religion, 177–78;
  and Christ, 71, 73–74, 78–80, 82–84,
  92–93, 95, 97, 98; and church, 98–
  100; and cross, 68–69, 93–94; early
  Christianity, 80–81; and faith, 98–99;
  and grace, 77; and Holy Spirit, 73–75,
  77, 81–82, 96–99; infant, 74–75, 79,
  99; interpretive key, 92–95; Jamaica,
  93–95; marginalization, 73; mystery,
  74–75; negative and positive, 79–80;
  new life, 75–85; participation in
  Christ, 76, 80, 82–83, 85, 87, 94–95;
  and Paul, 78–79, 80–81, 82, 87; redemption, 94; representation, 76–77;
  sacrament vs. symbol, 76–81, 82, 99;
  and salvation, 77; and solidarity, 71,
  84, 97–98; transformation, 93; and
  Trinity, 67, 81–82, 97–98; water, 76,
  77, 78, 79, 82, 96; white clothes, 94;
  and world, 68–69
Beloved Community, 28, 31, 182
Bible, 19, 35, 36, 110–11, 117, 155–56,
  158–59, 193

Black Atlantic, 3, 9
Black power, 28, 59, 123–24
Black theology, definition of, 116–17
Bland, Sandra, 185
Brown, Michael, 185

Caribbean: and Bible, 110–11; Blackness, 26–27, 112–13, 156–57; Black
  theology, 155–56; and Christ, 24,
  111–14, 117–18; and church, 23–25,
  109; class, 121; and colonialism, 20,
  21, 23, 25, 104, 114; and color, 15–16,
  36; and confirmation, 98; cross,
  112–13; decolonization, 25–26; and
  democracy, 16; and doctrines, 25;
  faith, 24; and King, 33–34; liberation,
  114–15; and missionaries, 19–21, 23,
  103–7, 108–9; new humanity, 26; and
  race, 14–15; salvation, 104–6; slavery,
  9, 15, 106; theology, 108–10, 155–57;
  and US, 11, 14–15
Caribbean Conference of Churches, 23
caste, 12–13. *See also* class
Charles V, 190
children, 45–46, 53, 63
Christology. *See* Jesus Christ
church: agent of transformation,
  167–69; and baptism, 98–100; Black,
  123, 133–35, 153–54, 163–67, 180; Black
  lives matter, 177–78; and Caribbean,

203

# Index of Scripture